**W9-AHJ-591**

# Life, Death & Bialys

By the same author

*Dog Stories*
*Misdemeanor Man*
*I Right the Wrongs*

# Life, Death & Bialys

## a father/son baking story

### Dylan Schaffer

BLOOMSBURY

Published by Bloomsbury USA, New York
Distributed to the trade by Holtzbrinck Publishers

All papers used by Bloomsbury USA are natural, recyclable products made
from wood grown in well-managed forests. The manufacturing processes
conform to the environmental regulations of the country of origin.

Library of Congress Cataloging-in-Publication Data

Schaffer, Dylan.
Life, death & bialys : a father/son baking story / Dylan Schaffer.—
1st U.S. ed.
p. cm.
ISBN-13: 978-1-59691-192-5 (hardcover)
ISBN-10: 1-59691-192-1 (hardcover)
1. Schaffer, Alfred Alan, 1930–2003. 2. Schaffer, Dylan.
3. Cancer—Patients—United States—Biography. 4. Fathers and sons—
United States—Biography. I. Title: Life, death, and bialys.
II. Title.

RC265.6.S275S33 2006
362.196'9940092—dc22
2006003185

First U.S. Edition 2006

1 3 5 7 9 10 8 6 4 2

Typeset by Westchester Book Group
Printed in the United States of America by Quebecor World Fairfield

For Guthrie and Cullen

# Prologue

*November 2002, evening*

My father calls from his home in South Carolina. I'm in California. He was born Alfred and later changed his name to Alan. His friends call him Flip.

"Sonny," he says.

"Hey, Poppala."

"How you?"

My father has a Ph.D. in history. Once he wrote plays. But as far as I know he's unaware there is a verb missing from this sentence.

"Surviving," I say.

"What are you doing in June?"

"I have no idea what I'm doing an hour from now."

"Don't be a wiseacre."

I'm at my computer. I search dictionary.com for *wiseacre*. Words, writing, politics, food—these are safe ground for us.

"Slang, derived from the Middle Dutch word for *soothsayer*," I report, attempting to divert him from whatever bizarre proposal he has in mind. The tactic fails.

"How about you and me take a bread-making class at the French Culinary Institute in New York?" he says.

"In June. That's seven months away."

"Right."

"I didn't know you were interested in bread."

"What's not to be interested?"

My parents divorced when I was five. I lived with my mother in New York. Her idea of dinner was two-day-old spaghetti with a dollop of cold Campbell's tomato soup. She also liked raw T-bone with green mint jelly. Flip, by contrast, has always been passionate about what he puts in his mouth. But he wasn't around to cook when I was growing up, so I lived on sugary breakfast cereal and bagels piled with deli meats and boxed chicken potpies.

I moved to Northern California in the late eighties and quickly fell for overpriced kitchen gadgets and cooking magazines and bags of Indian spices labeled in Hindi. I have learned to blanch string beans and to use a sushi knife and to brown a roux in a copper saucier.

A few months before my dad's call I'd started baking.

Flip and I often talk about cooking. But he never mentioned wanting to get into bread.

"Check out the Web site," he says. "The school is downtown. We'll stuff ourselves with pastrami and pickles." I can hear him salivating. I haven't heard my father so enthusiastic about anything in a long time.

I hang up and look around the Web site.

"Braided, sunny yellow challah bread . . . foccaccia, fragrant with herbs . . . crusty baguettes . . . and dense, chewy peasant loaves. There's nothing more tantalizing than home-baked breads. And in just one week at The FCI, you can discover the secrets of baking beautiful and distinctive artisan breads."

I must admit, it sounds pretty appetizing.

"As your distinguished Chef-Instructor works side-by-side with you, you will learn how to combine flour, water, yeast, salt and other ingredients to create a wide range of tastes and textures. You will discover how to adjust for variations in milling, the humidity of the kitchen, and even the weather. You will mix, ferment, punch down, shape, score, finish and bake your dough into delectable loaves. And your sense of accomplishment will grow."

I call back.

"You really want to do this?" I say.

"I already sent off a check. They give you a uniform and one of those paper hats."

"I'll go, but I'm not wearing the hat."

He ignores me.

"It'll be good for us. We haven't done something like this for a long time."

Actually, we've never done anything remotely like this. A few years after Flip left my mother he moved to Clemson, a small college town in South Carolina. I haven't spent more than a day or two alone with him in thirty years.

"The date again?" I say.

"June fifth."

"Of 2003?"

"Yes."

"What year is it now?"

"Dylan—"

"All right, relax. I'm writing it down. Baking with Pop, New York, June fifth."

I should mention that my father has metastatic lung and bladder cancer. According to the doctors, long before he can discover the secrets of baking beautiful and distinctive artisan breads, he will be dead.

# part one
# New York

*Als drait zich arum broit un toit*
It all comes down to bread and death

**—Yiddish proverb**

# chapter one

# On My Way, or Proof That Doctors Are Sometimes Wrong

*June 2003*

My wife's cat, Fisch, is missing. The cat is a mostly blind gray Siamese. Jennifer is in New Jersey with her sick grandmother. Her parting words were, "Give Fisch some love."

Not likely.

The cat and I share our creaky, badly insulated, not-exactly-earthquake-ready house in Oakland. I feed her and make sure she has a clean litter box. I help pay for her sky-high vet bills. But Fisch can't stand me. She won't let me get within ten feet. She whines for food outside my bedroom door before the sun rises. But when I trudge into the hallway, she has vanished. I've lived with the animal off and on for a decade and I could not pick her out of a lineup.

Now I have a more pressing problem. It's ten p.m. I'm supposed to fly off to New York the next morning to spend a week baking bread with my father, and the cat is not snuggled up in Jennifer's sweater drawer or curled into a corner under the bed. She's gone. I try shaking the treat bag, spreading catnip around the house, meowing, begging, and praying to a God who may or may not have jurisdiction in this case. If

Fisch disappears under my watch, my marriage is over. Come to think of it, this may be precisely what the cat has in mind.

After a night of desultory sleep, I call Jennifer. She will know what to do.

"I have to leave in ten minutes," I say.

"Where did you check?"

"I checked everywhere, twice. Maybe she got out."

"She's not an outdoor cat." This goes without saying. So basically what she means is, *You killed Fisch.*

"I feel sick."

"I'm sorry, Dylan. I can't take care of you now. Leave a note for Yvette." The neighbor charged with feeding the cat until Jen returns. "She'll come back."

Jen is the sort of doctor who works in a hospital and deals primarily with very sick people. She runs to *code blue* intercom calls and handles electrified paddles and yells "clear," like they do on *ER*. In the same circumstances I would sprint into the nearest bathroom and lock myself in a stall. I would stand on the toilet so no one could find me.

Jen became a doctor because she is curiously in touch with and uncomplaining about what is often called *reality*. Or perhaps she is that way because she became a doctor. Either way, she does not mince words and she does not offer false hope.

"I'm sorry. It's my fault," I say.

"That's true."


The plane ride is a turbulent hell. Before we take off the woman next to me, middle-aged, from Egypt, tells me she is going to New York to marry a man she has never seen, who she met on the Internet. The woman alternately weeps and pukes while the plane thrashes around the sky for five hours. After each hurling episode she looks at me, as if to wonder, *Could this be* your *fault?* I force a concerned smile. A few times the plane seems to be in a free fall and I think, *Now I will never know what happened to the cat.*

I take stock of my life, even though I know the plane probably won't crash, and I suspect I may be taking stock because that's what people do on crashing airplanes in movies. I'm rapidly approaching middle age. I've been a criminal defense lawyer for twelve years. I love my wife, though I sometimes have doubts that I can manage a lifelong relationship. My parents married six times—although they only married each other once. I can't decide about children. Why *do* people have children? I don't talk to my sister. My father is dying.

My parents met at New York University in the mid-fifties. My mother, whom everyone called Cookie, spent most of the year before she met my father in a mental institution. It often occurs to me that things might have turned out very differently if she'd stayed there.

Once I asked Flip what my mom looked like in those days. He shrugged his shoulders and said, "You know, she looked like a cookie." By which, I think, he meant she was cute, but not beautiful. She had a soft face and a prominent nose. When she smiled her cheeks gathered into taut knobs that must have been the target of elderly aunts looking for something satisfying to pinch. She had a large mouth and lips that were slightly too thin to contain her wide smile. Even then she had the beginnings of hollows around her eyes, which would grow grayer and deeper over the years.

Flip entered NYU after a stint in the army. The twenty-three-year-old freshman walked into class and parked next to the most attractive woman he could find. Her name was Phyllis Simmons and she was half a foot taller than my father's five feet and two inches. Phyllis sat to his left. He tried to talk to her, but she'd have nothing to do with him. This doesn't strike me as particularly surprising because Flip was funny looking. His best friend once said he looked as if he might have taken third place in a Woody Allen look-alike contest.

To Flip's right was my mother. Several months later they married. Cookie was seventeen.

After college my parents moved to Charlottesville, Virginia. Cookie went to medical school and produced my older brother, Cullen. Flip took a doctorate in history. Also he started to write plays. Cookie and Flip graduated and moved to East Lansing, Michigan. My father taught history at Michigan State and Cookie completed her internship.

The night I arrived, in August of 1964, Flip was in Rochester, New York, for the opening of his first play. We did not meet until I was several days old. His failure to appear at such a landmark event in my life provided early cause for resentment. Matters between us have been more or less the same since: He's gone and I'm mad.

My sister, Wendy, was born a year and a half later. I cannot say I remember her appearance on the scene, but I feel sure I wasn't happy about it. Given what happened later, I believe I would have been justified in passing her off to a neighbor. We spent much of the next twenty years squabbling, and, as I mentioned, now we have nothing to do with each other.

In 1967 we moved to New Rochelle, New York, about a half hour from Manhattan. Cookie finished her medical training and began a private psychiatric practice. Flip took a job teaching history at Lehman College in the Bronx, which is part of the City University of New York. My brother, Guthrie, was born in February of 1970.

Six months later, Flip walked out.


I've noticed that dens have gone out of style. Houses these days have family rooms, which tend to be expansive and sunny and open to kitchens and living rooms. Family rooms have sliding glass doors leading to backyards. In the seventies we had dens. Dens were paneled, with low ceilings, and deep, chocolate brown shag carpet. Dens had one closet filled with decaying board games and abandoned craft projects. Our den had one window that didn't open and shelves crowded with books. It smelled of cigarette and pipe smoke. Our den's closet housed hundreds of booklets into which Flip pasted coupons that used to accompany cigarette packages, and which, in large enough numbers, could be redeemed for semiworthless gifts such as monogrammed camping chairs and glow-in-the-dark phones.

My father worked in our den. He had a modular, glossy wood desk, and a metal cart topped with an electric typewriter the size of a Toyota Tercel. Flip sat in a swiveling desk chair with a lollipop orange seat cushion and backrest. Sometimes his friend Leon came over and they worked on plays together. I remember hearing Leon's high-pitched laugh late at night, while I was in bed in the room next door, tucked under my Peanuts blanket. I remember the thwack of the typewriter keys against the paper.

I was supposed to stay out of the den. But when Flip was out teaching I'd sit in his chair and spin myself around until my vision blurred, sucking the grassy smell of his pipe tobacco and cigarette butts into my nostrils.

I recall only one scene from the day my father moved out. It was August, shortly before my sixth birthday. I sat at our round white Formica kitchen table. Flip walked in carrying the orange swivel chair. My mother leaned against the counter with a defiant look on her face. He did not look at her or at me. He struggled with the chair, which was heavy and unwieldy. I did not open the door for him. I didn't want him to take the chair. I felt he should leave it for me, the same way I felt I should get a present when my parents returned from a trip. My father was leaving. I was owed.

At that time Cookie kept all the important details of her life—patient appointments, billing records, phone numbers—in a black, vinyl-covered date book. A few weeks after Flip left she misplaced the book. This is the first time I remember my mother going completely, out of control, scary nuts. *Paroxysm* is the right word, because more than just extreme anger, it suggests a fit—a display of fury that is as much physical as it is emotional.

She threw books and utensils and shoes at walls. She shrieked at our live-in housekeeper-nanny-cook for breaking a piece of china, and then she smashed the broken china some more. If we squabbled she ripped at our arms and legs and dragged us across the floor. She yelled at the cat for peeing on the floor and at herself in the mirror. Her screaming brought our neighbors out into their yards. For days Cookie stalked around ripping pillows off chairs, ransacking the same cabinets and drawers over and over again. I searched for the black vinyl-covered date book along with her and I searched when she was at work. But I couldn't find it.

Then *she* disappeared.

I arrived home from school one afternoon to find Cookie's mother, Ann, unpacking a suitcase in my parents' bedroom. My grandmother lived in Queens, so the suitcase was a surprise.

That night my dad, who had moved to the Bronx, came by the house. He sat on the living room couch, which made me nervous because Cookie said she didn't want him in her house.

My grandmother and father said Cookie had gone into the hospital because she wasn't feeling well. She needed rest. We wouldn't be able to see her for a while. I wondered why she couldn't rest at home, but I didn't ask. She was gone for weeks.

Over the years I became accustomed to Cookie's disappearances. She worked six days a week, sometimes fourteen hours a day. A string of women from the West Indies ran the house after Flip left.

When my mother was home, much of the time she was severely depressed and withdrew into her bedroom. I didn't intrude unless I had no other choice—to get a signature on a form or a check for some after-school activity. In that case I knocked gently. I didn't wait for an answer. Her voice was so weak when she was *down,* as she put it, that it was impossible to understand her from outside the door. I found her in bed, her hair oily and matted, her face the color of the cigarette ashes filling a plastic glass next to her bed. She was nearly unable to communicate. She seemed to resent my needs—scowling as she handed over the money or the signed paper.

When she wasn't working or hiding in her room, Cookie was threatening to leave permanently.

On weekend mornings Cookie sat with us while we consumed enormous quantities of Apple Jacks and Sugar Smacks and described, often without particular emotion, how she'd had it with taking care of us, how she hadn't bargained for raising four children alone, how she would go into her bathroom and swallow a bottle of pills and then we'd be Flip's problem. A week did not go by without Cookie warning, as I departed for school or a sleepover or for a visit with my dad, that I shouldn't be surprised to find her dead on the floor of her bathroom when I returned.

When he first left home Flip took out one of us, alone, once a month. He took me bowling or to the marina to see the sailboats. Afterward we went to Cook's, a cavernous, cafeteria-style eatery that had stations for different kinds of food. I'd walk back and forth among the burgers and tacos and pizza trying to make up my mind while Flip sat at a table smoking and drinking coffee. He never rushed me and I always chose the tacos.

At the back of the restaurant there was a game room with pinball machines and a car-racing game with a steering wheel and gas and brake pedals. I sat on his lap and took the wheel while he worked the pedals. When I looked back at him his cigarette was pinched between his lips, to one side. He squinted behind thick glasses as the smoke collected around his head. He'd say, "Come on. Look where you're going, Sonny," to get me to turn back to the game.

After a few years living in the Bronx, Flip left for Clemson.

I was nine. He never visited us in New York again. Instead, we flew south one school vacation each year and sometimes for a week in the summer. When I got older I spent my summers at camp and working, so I saw even less of him.

Since I went to college we've been in regular contact. We call. We visit a few times each year. But there remains a great distance between us. No matter how much time I spend with him as an adult, I can't forget that he abandoned me. He didn't fight for custody. He didn't live nearby. He left our house and then the state and made little effort over the years to be my father. He left me to be raised by a crazy woman.

When the plane touches down in Newark, I expect the passengers to applaud with enthusiastic relief. But they do not. I realize the cabin is nearly silent. The Egyptian woman in my row holds her head in her hands and mumbles what I assume are prayers. When we reach the gate and the pilot cuts the power the only sound is from three hundred seat belts unbuckling. The passengers are slow to rise and uncharacteristically polite. There is none of the usual scramble for cell phones or mad dash into the center aisle for overhead luggage.

Flip greets me in the airport lobby. I expect to see some sign that the cancer is taking its toll. But when I find him, he seems fine. He doesn't look like he's dropped any weight. His breathing is normal.

He is a Jewish Humpty Dumpty—scrawny legs, his body only slightly less wide than his five-foot-two-inch height, a couple of spare chins. Enormous, fleshy, pinkish ears jut from the sides of his head. Oversized trifocals with lenses as thick as an ice cube sit on a ledge at the top of his copious and slightly lopsided nose. He has an unshakable fear of dentists, so his teeth are stained and crooked. And despite three marriages, four children, seven decades, eight rounds of chemotherapy, and around nine hundred thousand cigarettes, Flip has a full head of mottled brown hair.

When I see my father I always have competing urges. I want to run to him and bury my face in his stomach and bawl into his shirt. I want to tell him how much I miss him and beg him not to go away again.

At the same time I am compelled to punch him in the face.

It's not a good feeling to want to hit your father. I think, sometimes—when I have a meltdown over a leak in the roof or find myself weaving riskily through traffic or yelling at my dogs for some minor offense—that this old rage sneaks out in destructive ways. I would like to patch up the old wounds. Perhaps I would be a less anxious and angry person. I've been to therapy. But I can't let it go.

I wrap my arms around him and squeeze. His mustache prickles the skin on my shoulder. I feel the damp under his shirt. And I begin to cry.

"It's all right, Sonny," he says. "I'm still taking nourishment."

"I know."

And I do. But it doesn't help.

# chapter two

# Suites

FLIP HAS A PENSION and a few hundred grand in the bank. He is also certain to be deceased in short order. So, while he has defied the odds and survived long enough to take an artisanal baking class at the French Culinary Institute in New York City, there's no chance he'll run out of money before he dies. Before the trip I urged him to book us into one of New York's upscale hotels for the week: the Ritz, the Four Seasons. He told me he'd handle it.

I become somewhat concerned when the cab heads into the Bowery, and then very concerned when it stops in a garbage-strewn alley. Dilapidated, sticker-laden vans line the curb—low-end rock-band cruisers. We weave through a gang of tattooed rockers loitering outside the hotel with cigarettes and forty-ounce beers in hand. Flip greets them like paparazzi, says "How you" several times in rapid succession, and moves relentlessly toward our destination.

I wheel our bags, behind him, into a lobby the size and smell of a bus station toilet stall. A man watching a baseball game is tucked safely behind bulletproof glass. My dad leans on a buzzer and the guy slides open the window.

He has no record of our reservation. My father elbows me aside and, his head only inches above the counter, takes charge.

"What's your name?" Flip says.

The man has a heavy accent, from the Middle East, I think.

"David."

Flip sticks his fat hand through the window and they shake.

"Nice to see you, David. My son is an attorney from California." I tense up. My father is forever suggesting I sue people on his behalf: corporations, politicians, neighbors. "I'm from South Carolina. We're attending an artisanal baking class at the French Culinary Institute."

He emphasizes the name of the school as if it were Harvard or the Sorbonne.

David looks less impressed than stunned.

Flip continues: "Obviously I did not choose this hotel because of its award-winning decor. I chose it because you're so close to the French Culinary Institute. I made the reservations over the Internet several months ago."

"Do you have a confirmation number, Sir?"

My dad pokes through his backpack and unearths a crumpled sheet of paper.

David studies the page for a moment. "Sir, please, you are in the wrong hotel."

"Son," my father insists, addressing David, not me, and grabbing back the sheet, "that's impossible."

I snatch the paper. Wrong hotel. He made the reservation for a partner establishment in Midtown.

Flip lays into David. I do not interrupt. I mean, this *could* be the last time he ever gets to yell at a clerk.

A manager type, with the same accent, hears the ruckus from an adjoining office and enters the fray. He bows slowly while my dad vents. Then he raises his hand to surrender.

"We're terribly sorry for the confusion, Sir. This is our mistake. We will be happy to put you in one of our suites."

Flip gives me a look that says, *You hear that? A little push and we get bumped up to a suite.*

Mind you, the place is called Suites Hotel, which suggests that *all* the rooms are suites. Nevertheless my father is beyond pleased with himself. He shakes both men's hands furiously and raps his index and middle finger twice on the counter, which is his universal sign for *we're done here.*

Our week together is less than two hours old. Already I've had to retip the driver after Flip got out of the cab because my dad gave him a third of an adequate gratuity. I've had to keep quiet about the choice of hotels, refrain from informing him that he screwed up the reservation, and hold my tongue about his contemptuous tone with the clerk.

My father is a short, fat, terminally ill bull in a world that is all china shop. It is best to avoid irritating the bull.

When he visits me in California he barrels off the plane, hugs me, and says, "Let's eat." I may not be hungry and I may have other plans, but neither is relevant. Initially, anyway, I want to make him happy. Last time he was in Oakland I took him to my favorite hole-in-the-wall Chinese place. There was a line. I explained that there's always a line because the food is great and well worth the wait. When we were at the head of the line, he glared at two diners he believed were dallying too long over their tea and said, in a loud voice, "Can you believe these people?" I asked him to try to relax, and he glared at me and said, "I'll relax when I'm eating."

He called the waitress *darling*. He looked at the menu and said, "I want the chicken with garlic sauce and the dumplings." Then he closed the menu and poked it into the waitress's midsection though her hands were occupied with taking our order. He did not say please or thank you. I said please and thank you for him. As always, he left too little tip. I made up the difference.

Flip basically likes to shop and to eat. He thinks movies are a waste of time, believes all music after Bach should be ignored, and has a similarly closed-minded view of art. Between meals and stores we talk about politics, upon which we agree. We stay away from family history. The few times I've asked him about his childhood he's said he doesn't remember. I've never pushed too hard on the subjects of my mother or how he felt about abandoning his kids.

If I tell my father Jen and I are not getting along or that I'm having trouble deciding whether to become a father, he changes the subject. If I tell him I'm depressed, which I am sometimes, he says, "I don't know how to help you. You'll just have to work it out."

For all of these reasons, our visits last for two or three days. We have a pleasant time. We do not fight. That is because right about the time I can't take another minute of churlishness and superficial chitchat, when I am at my limit of not being heard and not talking about why he wasn't around when I most needed him and not expressing my rage at his having left me with a woman he knew was totally unequipped to be a mother, he departs.

When Flip asked me to bake, I assumed he would be dead before the start of the class. I said yes without really thinking the whole thing through. He was terminally ill. He wanted to take the class. I didn't want to disappoint him.

As the date approached, I started to panic. Between the class and an intervening weekend, I'd be spending seven days with my father.

I did not know what would happen to us.


Flip took a job as chairman of the history department at Clemson University in 1974, which is when he left the New York area for good. The school paper ran a short piece on the event along with a picture of Flip. In it he looks like a producer of pornographic films. He was bearded and svelte, his button-down shirt wrinkled and opened at the top to reveal a thicket of chest hair. He wore a three-inch-wide belt and stylish glasses, round, and slightly too big for his face. His right leg was crossed over his left in a position that showed off too much crotch and his right hand rested on his knee, leisurely holding a cigarette. He looked as if he had just asked a woman up to his apartment for a wine spritzer.

I do not understand how a person who looked like this, who spoke with a thick New York accent, who was short and divorced and Jewish and had radical politics, ended up chairing a department at a large southern university.

It is not correct to say I had no father after Flip left New York. We talked on the phone. We wrote letters. I visited him in Clemson. It was more like my father had been exiled to a foreign country. I felt certain he still loved me. He said so. But I also knew that his circumstances prevented him from doing the things I saw other fathers do—attending school plays and graduations, throwing a ball around in the yard, telling my mother that she really shouldn't threaten to drive her car off a cliff every time she was in a bad mood.

Sometimes I visited my father in Clemson. Orange paw prints, the size of kiddy pools, dotted the highway that led into town. Flip said southerners were enthusiastic about sports, and about football in particular. The six-lane road, he said, was built to bring Tiger fans into and out of town on fall game days. Around the campus, nearly every available surface was covered with tiger paws. On Saturdays fans streamed up the road past my dad's house, toward the towering stadium called Death Valley, their foreheads and arms painted orange. We never went to a football game.

Flip's first house in Clemson was across the street from campus. It was stone and was freezing in the winter. My father refused to run the heater, believing that a benefit of moving south ought to be lower electricity bills. I slept in my down jacket.

The house was a block from Hardee's. In New Rochelle we had McDonald's and Burger King. But we did not have Hardee's. And Hardee's, along with charbroiled burgers, had biscuits. I'm sure there were better biscuits in the South, but there were none so close to my father's house. I don't eat biscuits now, and I'm not sure I really liked them then. I suspect I ate them for the same reason I wore a Clemson Tigers T-shirt when I went back to New Rochelle, and followed the Tiger's progress in the newspaper, though I didn't care about sports. Clemson was where my father lived.

Mornings, Flip left the house early and walked ten minutes to his office at Hardin Hall. I often went with him and sat in the common room where faculty and graduate students gathered to talk history and drink watery coffee and read week-old, mail-delivered copies of the *New York Times*. That people in Clemson had to wait days to get the news reinforced my sense that Flip had moved to a foreign country.

Flip loved Clemson. He said the biggest traffic jam was a few cars behind a stoplight. He marveled at the low property taxes though he didn't own a home until much later. He became an avid vegetable gardener. In New York, we had yards and trees and people who arrived in broken-down trucks once a month to mow the grass and trim the hedges. In New York, onions came from the A&P. Flip spoke fondly of compost and manure and seeds ordered through the mail.

My father played Frisbee with me in the yard, a cigarette in his left hand. The rule was that if he had to move more than one leg, the game was over. He would pivot, but he refused to travel to catch the disk. I learned to throw a Frisbee very accurately.


It is my mistake to assume that by *suite* the management of Suites Hotel has in mind anything beyond the plain meaning of the word, i.e., *a series of connected rooms used as a living unit.*

We have, indeed, a *series* of rooms; that is, two. The first is a kitchenette/salon/guestroom. The second is a bedroom. Each is crowded with furniture purchased, it appears, at a crack house. The bed seems designed to accommodate a person with severe spinal curvature. The TV works. The toaster does not.

The AC works brilliantly, which initially comes as a relief. Where I live, we have little humidity. Normally I avoid New York between May and September. The damp heat sucks the life out of me and I lose interest in all but ice cream. So, despite the otherwise shabby condition of our suite, I'm initially pleased to feel my nostrils contract with chilled air as we enter.

We soon discover that this air conditioner appears to have been designed for a Wal-Mart store. You could confidently keep your cryogenically preserved cat in our suite. I shut off the AC. Minutes later I am on the verge of heat exhaustion. I try the machine again, and the temperature swiftly plunges fifty degrees. There's no middle ground.

I back off the air conditioner a couple of steps and turn around to find my father, completely naked, carefully stowing the contents of his small suitcase in a dresser that, from the looks of it, has long doubled as an ashtray. I give him a look.

"What?" he says.

"You're not cold?"

"Not really." He *is* a hairy beast, my father, more chimp than human in that respect. But still, it's really cold. "Since I started the chemo my temperature regulation is a little off."

"Apparently."

He bends his torso over his skinny legs to stretch his back, although his stomach is so large that he doesn't make it very far.

"I gotta take a nap, Sonny. I'm spent."

"Are you nervous about the class?" I say.

"No. Why should I be nervous?"

"I don't know. *I'm* kind of nervous."

"What for?"

"I don't know."

"Wake me for dinner," he says.

Then he kneels into the bed and collapses onto his stomach. Before the bed stops groaning from the weight of him, Flip is out.

# chapter three

# We Arrive at FCI

IN THE EARLY EIGHTIES, Dorothy Cann Hamilton, a former Peace Corps volunteer and life-long epicure, opened the French Culinary Institute at 462 Broadway, at Grand, in New York's SoHo district. Ms. Hamilton got her MBA at New York University and, with her husband, co-owns a historic-inn-turned-restaurant in Connecticut. Among FCI's faculty are some of the most famous chefs in the world, including Jacques Pepin. Mr. Pepin was born in Bourg-en-Bresse. He was chef at the New York restaurants Le Cygne and Le Cirque, both of which earned four-star ratings from the *New York Times*.

I could go on. It is seven in the morning. I'm on my second Diet Coke, but the caffeine is kicking in too slowly. I could go on because Flip is sitting at a computer on the second floor of the D&D Deli and Grocery on Prince Street feeding me an unremitting stream of baking-class-related data from the Internet. At the same time he is eating breakfast: coffee with lots of cream and lots of artificial sweetener, and a toasted bialy with cream cheese and butter.

A bialy—short for bialystoker kuchen—is a small roll named for the city of Bialystock, Poland. It's about the size of a bagel. Rather than a hole, it has a depression in the middle that houses a mixture of diced onions and poppy seeds, or in some cases garlic. A bialy is chewy, like a bagel. Unlike a bagel, it is not boiled.

I ought to eat something. I may not have another chance for hours. But I'm not the least bit hungry. This has to do, at least in part, with the wolfish enthusiasm my father brings to his meal, to all meals.

When we visited Flip in his apartment in the Bronx, after he moved out, we ate McDonald's. Flip took a third of a Big Mac into his mouth at once. He held several fries in his fingers and dipped them in ketchup he'd squeezed out onto the paper burger wrapper. He dipped the fries in a bunch, covering his fingers in ketchup, and filled his mouth with fries and fingers together. When he was through, he took a long swig of coffee and mopped the grease from his face with a paper towel.

In Clemson, Flip learned to cook. He was fervent about knives, hoarded cooking magazines, and, after his satellite dish arrived, tuned into the Food Network day and night. Because he smoked for so many years, I don't think he actually tasted anything. Which may be why he seemed to inhale food rather than eat it. It may also be why, despite the money—for gadgets and ingredients ordered through the mail or purchased at obscure groceries in Atlanta—and energy expended, his food never tasted better than just fine.

But it's impossible not to appreciate his zeal. A few months before the baking class, Flip left a message on my answering machine asking me to call him right away. I assumed it was some sort of health crisis. Actually he'd just made a batch of shrimp scampi and he wanted to pass along the recipe. He said it was the best thing he'd ever made and he wanted to make sure to get it to me before something happened to him.

Some time ago, before the doctors pronounced him terminal, Flip offered me the following bit of fatherly wisdom: "Sonny," he said. "There comes a time in a man's life when food becomes more important than sex." He did not say when he reached that point. He did not illustrate the idea or expand upon it. It seemed like the sort of assertion that might well be true, but that I needn't ponder too closely. At least not yet.

But sitting with my father on the second floor of the D&D Deli on Prince Street, watching him poke the tip of his meaty tongue into his cream-cheese-and-butter-laden bialy, I see not only that he's crossed the sex-food barrier, but also that there's more to it. It's not just that food overtakes sex in importance; eating substitutes for lovemaking, food substitutes for lover.

And, it may well go without saying, the sight of my father pleasuring a bialy before seven in the morning hardly whets the appetite. He grunts, he moans, and when he's through the look on his face is distinctly postcoital.

"It says here *Jacques Pepin is everywhere at once.* You never know," Flip says, smiling impishly. "He might visit our class."

My father has a bit of a crush on Jacques, who makes regular appearances on the Food Network.

"What would you say to him?"

"I don't know," Flip says. "I'd be happy just to shake his hand."

"If he shows up, I'm going to ask him if he ever screwed Julia Child. Right in the middle of an episode on stuffed sole. Bent her over a chopping block, lifted up her apron and—"

Flip laughs with his mouth full. Coffee and bits of bialy dribble down his stubbly beard. I don't hide my disgust. For the first time today I feel fully awake.

Flip and I walk the three blocks to FCI. The school, along with its highly regarded restaurant, L'Ecole, is housed in a large building in the heart of SoHo. Pricey galleries and clothiers line the streets nearby. On the way we wind through a stream of dazzling, long-legged women and dark-haired, strapping, vigilantly coifed men. They all look as if they're heading to a photo shoot.

For the first time in fifteen years, since I graduated from law school, it's the first day of school again—same fear of not fitting in, same uncomfortable mix of shyness and yearning to be liked.

A mob of students, most in their twenties, loiters around the FCI entrance smoking and drinking enormous cups of coffee. They wear checkered pants and white coats and puffy chef's caps. They are extravagantly pierced and tattooed. Their faces are pale. They do not look like they've slept well in weeks and I wonder if it's a good idea for them to be handling cleavers and hot oil. But I don't say anything or even make eye contact, because they're an intimidating lot. Flip and me, we're dilettantes, tourists in the land of cooking professionals. These people are lifers, loading up on caffeine and nicotine before they tackle a side of beef or a recalcitrant puff pastry. I keep my shoulders hunched and my head bent over in an apologetic manner as we push past them into the building.

Flip informs the first person we find that we're here for the baking class. The man passes by without a glance. We continue on and end up in a noxious-smelling loading dock crammed with a hundred clear plastic bags of restaurant garbage. The men there speak Spanish to one another. I turn back, but I hear Flip try for help in what sounds like German to me. He gets nowhere. We pass two large kitchens that service L'Ecole, pausing for a few moments to observe senior students prepping for lunch. The atmosphere is no-nonsense. A student holding a chef's knife the length of my arm glances over his shoulder at us and returns to work. He looks as if he might have been there all night, chained to the stainless steel workstation.

We climb a stairwell and find a woman with a clipboard. She claims to know nothing about a baking class and directs us to the office. Thirty seconds later we are again hopelessly lost, roaming an empty hallway that leads to another hallway. I tell Flip I think we should return to the hotel. He ignores me.

Eventually we discover we'd passed the office twice already. It was, on those occasions, unoccupied and locked, hardly a surprise since my father insisted on arriving at the school forty minutes early. Now the door is propped open. I enter, gingerly, having become accustomed to feeling we don't belong, or that we may be in the wrong place entirely. Flip barrels in behind me and pushes me out of the way.

An attractive young woman dressed for office work darts out from behind her desk. She, too, has a clipboard, which she clutches to her chest with one arm while extending the other.

"You must be Dr. Schaffer." The greeting is exuberant. Flip gives me an *I told you so* look. "We're so pleased you could make it."

For the next ten minutes the woman and my father have the sort of conversation that would make perfect sense if Flip were a wealthy alumnus who'd hinted he was contemplating a large donation. Despite the hour, she is extraordinarily sociable, pressing Flip for all sorts of information—about his work, family, interest in cooking, and so forth. She seems genuinely interested, smiling at appropriate times, maintaining eye contact, ignoring her phone.

The exchange worries me. A couple of months earlier I'd phoned the school and spoken to someone in charge. My dad didn't appear to be going downhill quickly, but Jen led me to believe that could change quickly. It seemed the considerate thing to explain the situation in case we had to cancel at the last minute. But I asked the person not to share the information with anyone, particularly not the baking class chefs.

Either this woman is both implausibly friendly and well informed about incoming students, or she knows my father is dying. If that's the case, and Flip finds out, I'm in serious trouble.

"*She* was nice," Flip says as we leave the office.

"Mmmm."

We head off to another office to take care of our bill and we each receive our official artisanal baking class gear, *to wit*: one pair of drawstring pants, one baker's coat, two aprons, one neckerchief, one plastic name tag, one large sheet of white paper for indeterminate use, one plastic-bound book titled *Introduction to Artisanal Bread Baking,* one yellow plastic bench scraper, two dish towels, and one thermometer.

"What's this for?" I say, holding out the sheet of paper.

"That's your hat," Flip says, as if I am a total moron.

Perhaps if I were not his son Flip's know-it-all tone would not bother me. But as it is, I find it upsetting and confusing. He often sounds angry when I'm unable to understand something he's explaining.

My response, now, as usual, is to make a joke.

"It looks more like something to wrap meat in."

He twists the sheet into a tube and fits it over his head. He looks very much like someone with a large tube of white paper on his head.

"How does it stay on?" I say.

"You staple it."

"I forgot my stapler. Does that mean I can go home?" He does not respond. "There's no top? What if sparks fly out of the oven and light my hair on fire?"

"Keep it up," he warns.

Along with our uniforms we get the access code to the locker room where we're to deposit our street clothes and emerge looking like bakers. Flip punches in the code and tries the door, but it doesn't budge. He tries again, but has no luck. A wave of frustration rushes from his face to his hands, which begin to quiver.

"Pop," I say, laying my hand on his. "It—"

"What?" He barks back.

"Nothing."

A student opens the door from within. We enter and Flip disappears to find his assigned locker, mercifully distant from my own.

The changing area seems designed to cause maximum anxiety. It is cramped, jammed with rows of lockers and crowded with students rushing to get to class. The din is unbearable. Students shout at one another over the rows, toss around kitchen equipment, and slam locker doors. Meanwhile, the aisles are so small and the lockers crammed so close together that I have to stand around for minutes before I can reach mine. The room smells like a wool ski sock worn for a week without washing.

When I was in high school the locker room was a violent place. Not being an athlete, I was a target. The FCI locker room may be less overtly sadistic and criminal, but it has much the same macho, thuggish air. Students recount deviant, alcohol-fueled sexual escapades at the top of their lungs. A raspy-voiced man from across the room, referring to one of the chefs, says, "If he starts with me today I'm gonna julienne his thumb."

When I finally reach my locker, my neighbor, emaciated, boyish-looking, possibly psychotic, grumbles to himself incoherently while organizing a black toolbox filled with sharp kitchen implements. He looks up at me.

"How's it going?" I say.

"Just don't leave your shit around. Unless you *want* someone to fuck with it."

He slams his locker, then his gearbox, and pushes out of our row.

After changing I wait for my dad in the hallway outside the locker room. When he emerges I see that he's entirely missed how to wear the apron. It looks more like a bib. I help him fix it.

"You know," I say. "You could make pretty good money as the Pillsbury Doughboy."

"What?" Age and cancer treatments have dulled Flip's hearing.

"I said, you look stunning."

And in a way, he does. The outfit thins him out a bit, and the hat, although it's still just a stapled tube of butcher paper, is surprisingly dignifying. Flip paid extra to have his name stitched on his jacket and now that I've helped him with the apron you might mistake him for a wizened chef, a man who has earned his wrinkles sweating over grill stations and dismembering steer.

"You, too, Sonny."

# chapter four

# In the Baking Room

WHEN WE FINALLY reach the baking room we see several other bread students milling around uneasily in starched uniforms and ridiculous-looking paper hats. Flip, with a string of "How yous" and handshakes, breaks the ice. I follow, like a sidekick.

The bread kitchen at FCI smells like being four and wet from the rain and coming inside and pressing your face into your mother's apron after she's spent a morning baking cookies. Not that my mother, despite her name, ever baked a cookie in her life. But that's how the room makes me feel— safe and content. The aromas are so old and so complex as to be almost narrative. I smell pecan pie, but, like, pecan pie waiting on the counter while I eat my just-out-of-the-oven calzone stuffed with fresh basil, mushrooms, and feta and drink my Heifeweisen.

The room is thirty feet by thirty. White, square acoustic tiles cover the fifteen-foot-high ceilings. Fluorescents, nestled into the ceiling and walls, cast a merciless, shadowless glow into every nook and cranny. Matching sets of four bare wood butcher-block tables, pushed together, provide two enormous work surfaces. Though they are not for sitting, these are called *benches*. Suspended from the ceiling, about four feet above, are twin, room-length power strips. Glossy white, brick-shaped ceramic tiles cover the walls, which suggests the room may once have been an enormous bathroom.

Labeled rolling bins of every dry good you could possibly use to bake bread fit snugly beneath the worktables—all-winter white flour, rice flour, sugar, buckwheat, medium rye, whole rye berries, fine whole wheat, coarse whole wheat, all purpose, several kinds of high protein bread flours with names like Sir Galahad and Sir Lancelot, rolled oats, coarse corn meal, milk powder, nine grain mix, white flour with wheat germ and bran, rye flakes, seminola, durum, sea salt.

The gear of the artisanal baker lines the four sides of the room. Starting at the door and rotating clockwise: sinks, scales, stoves, more sinks, refrigerators, flour storage room, a stack of ovens, a retarding room, another stack of ovens, cooling racks, a liquid levain machine, spiral mixers, more sinks, back to the door. Shelved above and below, and on wheeled carts scattered around the room, are all manner of baking accoutrements: buckets, bowls, bins, pots, pans, rollers, peels, spices, fire extinguishers, burn kits, rolling pins, knives, cloth-lined rising baskets, and lots of other stuff I can't identify.

The students, ten besides Flip and me, seem like a serious bunch. There's no chatter. But still the room is noisy—exhaust fans whir, refrigerators buzz, the levain machine churns. Add to this the mixers and faucets and baking activity and I see it's going to be a loud week.

I consider saying, "All dressed up and nothing to bake," or something equally idiotic, but I do not. We sit on stools around one of the benches and stare at our pristine recipe books, fingering thermometers and dishtowels. My father drums the nails of his right hand against the bench at two-second intervals.

"So, how are you feeling about this whole thing?" I say, discreetly, to avoid engaging any of the other students.

"Pretty good. Not bad. Ready to bake," he says, louder than me. Two students lift their heads and smile.

"Are you interested in anything in particular?" This is from Dave,* who is about fifty, short, bony, bushy eyebrows, thick, black-rimmed glasses, and no lips at all.

"I gotta learn to make bialys," my father says after shaking Dave's hand and introducing himself, but not me.

"I don't think that's on the list," Dave says. Dave sounds like he knows what's on the list.

"You're serious?" Flip says.

"Not that I saw," Dave says.

"That's outrageous."

"I'm sure you'll bring this up with the authorities at the first opportunity," I say.

"I certainly will," Flip says. "I'm not leaving New York without being able to make a decent bialy."

An extremely attractive woman, tall and slender with curly black hair tied up in a bun and long fingers, shakes Flip's hand and then mine. Her name is Abby. Her eyes are dark blue and her eyelashes are an inch long. She tells Flip if he needs backup on the bialys thing, she's game.

---

*The participants in the June 2003 Artisanal Baking class paid good money to learn how to make bread. They did not pay to end up in a book. Without exception, they were very nice to my father and me. For these reasons, and because I intend to make fun of one or two of them, the names of my classmates, and identifying details, have been changed.

Abby wants to know where I'm from. I tell her Flip dragged me all the way from California, where the weather, at present, is a perfect seventy-five degrees, with no discernible humidity.

She smiles and says to Flip, "That's so nice of you, to invite your son to the class."

He leans toward Abby and half whispers, "Well, I'm a very good father."

Except for the fifteen years I most needed him, during which he wasn't a father at all, he's not totally off base. He recently bought me a microwave oven, which was nice.

Cookie was a good mother, too.

When I was little, and she wasn't so depressed that she couldn't communicate, we spent the mornings snuggling. Although she was a small woman she had an enormous platform bed piled with pillows and down comforters. My siblings and I jumped around like the bed was a trampoline, pummeling one another with pillows. She laughed with us. And then, reliably, she cried. We stopped playing and hugged her, each clinging to a different limb.

Sometimes she cried about a financial crisis. Sometimes it was a breakup. She always said she didn't know what she would do without us. We were all that was left in her life that had any meaning. If she didn't have to provide for us she'd just go off by herself and die.

Sometimes she would read to us before bed. But reading time was a bit of a mixed bag because often Cookie would start to cry in the middle of *Where the Sidewalk Ends* or *Harold and the Purple Crayon*. She was exhausted. She didn't know if she could go on. I was just seven or eight, but

I felt responsible for her exhaustion, guilty about keeping her up, to blame that she had to work so hard.

Like all good mothers, Cookie took an active interest in my social life. Twice during my early teen years I dated girls my mother had seen in her psychiatric practice. It was Cookie, not my girlfriends, who told me. She felt I should know about their emotional problems before I became too attached. So, she told me about the father who couldn't keep his hands off his daughters and the drunk mother and the anorexic sister. She said Marie was depressed and I should be sure to report back if she said anything about killing herself. Beth, she warned, would certainly have to be institutionalized at some point. I could date whomever I liked, but she felt I should have the facts.

My mother also took us on nice vacations. For example, for some time Cookie dated a wealthy married man. When we saw the man we were not supposed to tell him we knew he was married. Which would have been easier if Cookie hadn't spent hours at the dinner table and in the TV room loudly mourning the fact that she was in love with a married man. The married man bought her a sports car, which I thought was pretty cool. Also, the married man happened to be one of her patients, but that didn't seem to be a problem.

When she wasn't crying over him, she told us all about the married man. She said he was wonderful and sensitive and kind. She told us about his fancy house and love for wildlife. She said she didn't know what would happen with the married man's wife, or his family, but she really wanted us to meet him. So we all went to Disney World and to the Everglades. We stayed in a fancy hotel and drove around in a convertible.

Another time she took us to Europe. Except for the day she got caught stealing a handmade quilt from a fancy hotel in Amsterdam, it was a great trip. The funny thing is that Cookie wasn't embarrassed; she was furious. The concierge stopped her in the lobby. He asked to search our luggage. My mother angrily refused and sent us to wait outside. I knew it was the quilt because I'd seen her stuff it into a suitcase. I'd even asked her not to steal the quilt. Ten minutes later, in the cab, Cookie fumed at how stupid they were for refusing to let her have the silly blanket. Now she would never stay at the hotel again.

On another trip, this time to Israel, we were at the Dead Sea. Cookie thought I should have the experience of swimming in such salty water. I really did not want to swim in the Dead Sea because I had a nasty case of athlete's foot and the skin between my toes was cracked and raw. I figured it might hurt to swim in salt water. I explained this to Cookie but she wouldn't budge. I had to swim. I went in with my sneakers on, but the water still got to my toes and burned horribly. My sneakers were ruined and floating on top of the water wasn't as impressive as Cookie promised.

Around the beginning of junior high I got tired of hearing my mother whine about how miserable her life was, how the only reason she went on living was because she, unlike Flip, had committed to taking care of her children. I got tired of being responsible for her pain, of watching her pull us out of friendships and family gatherings because of her resentments and paranoia. I'd had enough of her berating waiters and stealing from hotels and not being a mother. I was sick of her unremitting suicide threats.

So, I spent the rest of my time in New Rochelle in the dog-house. The cool thing about living in the doghouse is that no matter how depressed or busy or overwhelmed by life my mother was, I could always get her attention.

Our fights always had the same arc, as if the whole thing was theater.

I stayed out too late or got sent to the principal's office or whacked my sister, who almost always deserved it. Cookie got home at eight, having worked twelve hours. You could hide a quarter in the bags under her eyes. Cullen was already in college. Wendy and Guthrie rushed into the kitchen to greet her. Wendy or our nanny-housekeeper-cook, who was making Cookie's dinner, informed my mother of my offense. Usually the sin du jour was one of a string of relatively minor screwups. So, most likely, I stayed out too late *and* got sent to the principal *and* whacked my sister. But I was not a delinquent. I got good grades, had nice friends, was modest in my use of illegal drugs, and beat up on my younger siblings only when absolutely necessary and never to the point of permanent injury.

Cookie, severely depressed and insanely overworked, lacked the perspective to see that my sins were trivial, that I wasn't really a bad kid, that I probably just needed some mothering. The woman was an expert in child behavior. You might think she would have been aware of the doghouse syndrome.

After hearing of my small transgression she marched into my room, her three-inch heels clicking down the hardwood-covered hallway. She yelled at me from the door, first, always, that she shouldn't have to deal with this, the minute she walks in the house, after working twelve hours. "I'm tired. I've had enough. I can't take it anymore."

I got off my bed to greet her at the door. I tried to tell her my side of the story. There was always another side.

She shrieked, "I don't care. I don't care. I'm not listening." She stuck her fingers in her ears. "For once I want to come home and not hear Dylan, Dylan, Dylan. You can't always be the center of attention." Her arms swung around her body wildly. She leaned far over her heels, like she might topple forward.

I yelled, she shrieked. She said she wouldn't pay another dime for anything. No acting lessons. No summer camp. I couldn't go out with my friends. She would take my stereo, my records, my new sneakers.

I told her to go to hell or worse. She cursed at me. Our bodies were inches apart. Her saliva hit my face while she screeched. I pushed her out of my room. She told me to keep my hands off her, to never touch her again. I kept pushing. I told her to stop screaming at me. She stumbled down the hallway, grabbed whatever she could—a book, a phone, a pewter bowl, and threw it at me. I threw it back and locked myself in my room. She pounded on the door, screaming, crying, "No more, no more, you're not going to treat me like this anymore." Eventually she retreated to her room.

In a short final scene, an hour or two later, one of us would go to the other, apologize, hug, cry. We always ended up agreeing that we didn't want to fight. But we never figured out how not to.

The last time I lived with Cookie was during my junior year of college. I had an internship in New York. We argued constantly. At some point my mother decided she wanted me out of the house.

I had been studying for months to prepare for the law school entrance test. Cookie chose to kick me out the morning of the exam. She called the police and had them send over an officer who stood over me while I packed my bag, led me outside, and told me if I came back I'd be arrested. I took the LSAT. Then I went to my friend's house. Late that night I went home to get some things I'd left behind. I knocked at the front door. Cookie called the police. I told her to let me get my things and I'd leave. She had me arrested. It was several years before we spoke again.

Actually, Cookie was a lousy mother. But at least she tried. Flip just walked away.

chapter five

# We Learn a Thing or Thirty-Two

AN HOUR AFTER BAKING CLASS begins I'm extremely sorry I came to New York.

I have the same too-much-chocolate, faintly nauseated and uncomfortable-in-my-own-skin feeling I had during my one semester of calculus. At first I do my absolute best to keep up. But soon I feel like banging my forehead on the workbench. There's no way I'm ever going to understand any of it. Deep down I know I'd be smart to strip off my paper chef's hat, wish them all good luck, and depart.

A kind-looking, soft-spoken German man named Hans leads the class. We call him, simply, Chef. He is perhaps fifty, with forearms the size of adolescent oaks. He has a baker's face and belly, round and a bit doughy. He has long eyelashes, a closely cropped graying mustache, a pinched nose that slopes into a small knob at the end, and a fading tattoo of a compass on his left arm from his days in the German navy.

Hans wheels over a white board. This morning, he says, we are going to learn some basic skills, and bake the core breads of the French artisanal baker: the baguette and the bordelaise. At his direction, we open our recipe books to page forty-three, which contains the heading: "Baker's Percentage." A baker's percentage, he explains, is the method by which we determine how much of each ingredient we use to make each batch of dough.

I whisper in my dad's ear, "People usually call that a *recipe.*"

But as I turn forward in the book, a page, and then another, I am stunned by a thicket of math and grids and formulas in bold type with unfamiliar acronyms, like $AQF = TAF \times \%F$. When I return to the lecture, I am hopelessly, helplessly lost; so lost that I'm afraid to raise my hand because I would have no idea what to say, other than, "Heh?" I look at Flip, who must seem to the other ten students to be following attentively. I know better. My father is even more innumerate than me. Also he's about fifty percent deaf. So, I'm positive Flip isn't hearing what he wouldn't understand anyway.

When Hans concludes the baker's percentage discussion he encourages us to try some of the impenetrable exercises in the book in our free time. Several wisecracks come to mind, but the grave looks on my classmates' faces keep me quiet.

Except for Abby, whose bun is coming undone and whose eyes I've noticed shifting around the room during Hans's lecture. I risk a glance, making clear with my wide eyes and my pursed lips that I'm lost. She makes a gun with her forefinger and thumb, puts it to her temple, and fires.

Hans tells us to turn to the first bread recipe, straight dough baguette. According to the book, this recipe serves the following "OBJECTIVES: 1. To prepare straight dough and its derivatives. 2. To understand the concept of *autolyse.* 3. To demonstrate proper shaping skills of all members of the baguette category."

I'm momentarily comforted. It's not that I have any idea what *autolyse* is. But at least this bit is expressed in words, not numbers or formulas. And the objectives seem to be relatively straightforward. We make the dough; we learn to shape it. I have done both of these things before, at home.

Hans ignores the objectives entirely and begins a lecture on a subject that is nowhere in the book and has to do, again, with numbers and formulas. This time it's something called *friction factor.*

Temperature, in baking serious bread, is king. If the dough comes out of the mixer at the proper temperature—in most cases seventy-seven degrees—it's destined to cooperate for the rest of its short life. But, Hans warns, when you dump eight kilos of flour and water and other ingredients into an industrial spiral mixer—which looks like your basic Kitchen Aid stand mixer on steroids—and crank it up for several minutes, you end up heating the dough far above its ideal temperature. The skilled baker manages this problem by determining the friction factor of the mixer, taking into account the temperature of the rising environment, and adjusting the entry-level temperature of the water accordingly.

I must confess that it was not until much later in the class that I *heard*, let alone *understood*, this definition of friction factor. Now, instead, I'm stuck on the quantities Hans scribbles on the white board: 5,000 grams of flour; 3,100 grams of water; 50 grams of yeast. Although my metric skills are not totally trustworthy, I've been representing drug dealers long enough to know that 5,000 grams is the same as five kilos and five kilos is a hell of a lot of cocaine, or flour, or whatever.

I raise my hand. "How many loaves of bread would that make?"

Hans says it depends on the size of the loaf you're shaping; but for a baguette, about thirty loaves per batch.

I eat a lot of bread. Sometimes I eat bread several times in a day. But still, thirty loaves seems a bit excessive. I could probably make do with, say, twelve, even if I were planning to give some away.

When I glance around the room, I don't see anyone else looking perplexed. The answer seems to make perfect sense to them. I tap Flip on the shoulder.

I whisper, "Why would anyone want to make thirty loaves at once?"

He pauses for a moment and then says, "Good question."

Sometimes I love my father, despite his many faults, simply for sharing my genetic material.

I lean into his left ear. "No one else seems to be bothered that these recipes are institutional-sized. And look at the mixers. I couldn't fit one of those things through my front door. Are you sure we're in the right class?"

"So ask," he says, suddenly irritated.


I am greatly confused. About baker's percentages and friction factors and outsized recipes, yes. But it hardly ends there. I am confused about preferments—poolish and sponge and biga. I am confused about milling techniques and protein percentages. And presoaking and retarding and scoring. And dough strengtheners and dough conditioners. And mold inhibitors and enzymes and oxidizing agents. And oven conditions. I'm even confused about things I really, really thought I understood before I arrived at FCI. For example, I am now mystified by water.

After the introductory lecture I feel the class is a big mistake. Before, making bread was something I gave very little thought to and, a few times a year, enjoyed doing. Now, to my chagrin, I understand I haven't been baking at all. I know what I *don't* know, which means I know what I have to learn. Mastering even the basic skills of a baker will involve an extraordinary output of intellectual and physical energy. And for what? It's not like before, when I was *not baking*, I was frustrated by my lack of artisanal skills. I was ignorant, and blissfully so.

"What's wrong?" Flip says.

"What the hell are we doing here?" I say. "Do you have any idea what he's been talking about for the last hour?"

Flip is hardly the sort who would admit bewilderment, but Hans calls the class over to one side of the room before he has a chance to answer.

Hans demonstrates how to operate the enormous spiral mixers. After loading the large stainless steel drum with ingredients—translated from the metric: eleven pounds of flour, seven pounds of water, and a whole lot of yeast and salt—he punches numbers for speed and time into a keypad, drops the splashguard, and off it goes. It mixes, it kneads. It even takes a break—the *autolyse*—if you tell it to.

While the mixer churns, Dave, whose questions account for ninety-five percent of the total asked, asks, "How much do these go for?"

Excellent question. I was thinking I might have to pick one up next time I have a hundred and eighty-four friends over for pizza.

"Maybe five thousand," Hans says, in his lightly accented English.

The steel mixing arm is as thick as the grip end of a baseball bat. Next to the keypad is a large red button. Hans warns us to hit it if the machine gets a hold of one of our legs.

"It just wants to mix, you know," he says, chuckling. "It doesn't know what goes inside."

When the mixer cuts off, Hans pulls out the drum with one hand and dumps its contents into a well-oiled plastic tub. Before he covers it we take turns poking and prodding and smelling our first batch of mixed dough. It is nothing like the stiff, dry dough balls I've made at home. It looks like the pale, toddler son of the Blob. It is sticky and pliable. It smells musky sweet, like dried shitakes soaking in water.

I ask if I can taste it. Hans pulls off a bit. I put it in my mouth. It's smooth, like the outside of a grape, but also soft, like wilted spinach. It crackles between my teeth.

The next stop on the kitchen tour is a stack of six ovens, each about ten inches high, which occupies a corner of the room. With the punch of a few buttons the oven cranks to six hundred degrees. Another button injects a stream of steam into it, which, Hans says, helps crisp the outsides of breads like baguettes. Pull a black knob out of the oven and it quickly releases the moisture. When Hans pops open the door on one of the ovens a wave of dry heat hits us and we all take a step backward.

Hans doesn't seem to be bothered by the oven. He stands with the side of his face inches from the open door, lecturing about the effects of humidity, temperature, and altitude on baking.

He crosses the room and invites us, two by two, into the retarder, a slightly refrigerated and heavily humidified room where certain kinds of dough sit overnight to develop flavor before they go into production. It's nice inside, damp, cool. It's quiet, in marked contrast to the baking room. And it's dark. The only light comes through tinted windows on the doors. Flip and I, alone inside the retarder, poke around a bit, filling our noses with the chilly air and verdant, beery smell of rising dough.

When Flip tries to exit I put my hand on the door.

"I want to tell you something."

"What?" he says, annoyed.

"It's not easy for me to say this."

He turns back to look at me.

"I've always suspected you were retarded," I say.

"Are we done?"

"Admit that was funny."

He stares at me.

"There's one other thing."

"Dylan."

"I think I'm falling in love with Abby."

I should mention here that along with my wife's firm grasp of reality goes a sensible view of the ways of the heart. That is, we've been together for a long time, and she expects and accepts that we will both find others whom, under unmarried circumstances, we might well like to date. I will certainly tell her all about Abby, and she will tell me, as she always does, to enjoy myself. Which means, enjoy looking, not touching.

"Jesus, enough already," he says.

"Do you think she likes me?"

I let him push open the door, and I follow him out, but the few minutes in the retarder convince me it is the right place to spend most of the week at FCI.

# chapter six

# We Meet Our Classmates, and Our Classmates Meet Us

WE RETURN TO our stools. Hans tells us a little about himself and then introduces his assistant, Chef Catherine. Catherine is a small woman in her early thirties with a distinctly Mediterranean look: coffee-colored hair, olive skin, wide, brown, vivid eyes, a prominent, sensibly sloping nose. She gasps slightly before speaking, unable to contain her exuberance, especially when it comes to baking.

For the most part I don't catch Hans and Catherine describing their baking credentials because I'm distracted by the absence of bread on the six-foot-wide, five-foot-high, six-tiered chrome cooling racks to the right of the stack of bread ovens. This morning I've personally witnessed the chefs pull twenty loaves out of the ovens with long wooden peels and slide them onto the racks. As far as I know none of the students in the artisanal baking class has had a moment to eat any of this bread. We've had no visitors. Yet the racks are almost bare.

I see, now, that behind the racks is not wall, but a door, and that the door is open, and that anyone passing through the hallway outside the class can easily help him or herself to a few of our baguettes.

I think of the right way to convey this security breach to Hans. But before I can raise the alarm I see an older man in a chef's uniform walk up to the nether side of the racks and help himself to the remaining loaves. He makes no attempt at stealth. Indeed, he whistles, attracts Hans's attention, and, despite the several baguettes clutched under his arm, receives a friendly wave from our leader.

Hans cuts slices from a baguette, plates them along with a slab of butter and a heaping of raspberry jam, and sends it around the table. He asks us to introduce ourselves and explain why we're taking the class.

When the platter reaches me I smear butter on a slice and bite down, twisting it over until it comes apart. First I taste the salt and fat from the butter, but then the bread comes through. It's sweeter and lighter than I'd imagined, not as sour as the bread I'm used to. It's chewy, like a bite of medium-rare rib eye.

Flip's turn to speak arrives before mine. I'm curious what he'll say about what we're doing here. Could this be the moment he'll reveal himself? Will he tell this group of strangers that he'll be lucky to make it to his seventy-third birthday in October? That he's here to say good-bye to New York? That, for him, this class is about more than bread; that he's writing his life's epilogue?

Flip says he's a retired history professor from South Carolina who's here to learn to bake. In particular, he would like to learn to make bialys. My stomach clenches.

Hans says we will do bagels, but there won't be time for bialys. He says this in a kind way, but leaves no room for discussion. I look over at Abby. She shrugs but doesn't second Flip's motion.

First Flip looks stern, and I think he might make a stink. Then he screws up his face and says, "Bagels? *Blech.*" In Flip's case, this is about a tenth of a stink.

He gets a big laugh.

Then it's my turn. These sorts of small group speaking moments always throw me. I ought to have thought of something to say while the others introduced themselves. But I was too busy obsessing—first over the theft of our baguettes, and then over what Flip might say. Why am I here? I have no idea. Because my father is dying and he asked me to come. Suddenly even the idea of my own name spoken aloud is nearly unbearable; it's a reminder that my days as Flip Schaffer's son are numbered. And it's a reminder of how much time he squandered along the way. I clear my throat, buying myself a few moments.

"I'm Dylan and"—I point to Flip—"I'm his son. When my dad told me he was going to learn to bake bread, I immediately signed up. Basically I'm here to make sure he doesn't set the building on fire."

The knot in my throat loosens.


Hans divides us into three baking teams, four students each. He explains that each day, when we arrive in the morning, we should consult the white board where we'll find our baking assignments, which include mixing three different varieties of baguette dough and preparing dough for bordelaise, a large, heavy, dense, dark-crumbed French bread that makes a tasty sandwich as well as an effective weapon.

The teams are also responsible for scaling and shaping the various batches of baguette and bordelaise—in other words, taking dough that has been through its first rise, cutting it up into small portions, shaping those portions into loaves, putting them into a second rise, and then baking the loaves. Finally, each day one team is assigned to clean out the liquid levain machine at the close of business.

The good news is Flip and I are not on the same team. Baking bread is a tense, exacting business. We work in close quarters near ovens set to five hundred degrees. Knives and dangerous machinery fill the room. Best to share the experience at a safe distance.

The bad news is that my father seems to have landed in the cool, attractive, talented group while mine appears to be the team most likely to destroy one of the school's pieces of expensive equipment.

Flip's teammates include the aforementioned Abby, who, I've noticed, laughs at my jokes. She is married, and I am married, but I would not have minded a few days of invigorating flirtation.

Then there's an elegant, gentle-voiced, fiftyish woman named Laurie. And Joe. After the first few skills exercises it becomes clear that Joe, short and round, with a nose that has certainly been broken more than once and hands the size of catcher's mitts, is a professional baker. I would like to know what he is doing in this class, but Joe doesn't speak much English. I gather only that he is employed by or related to someone on Team Two. But anyway, Joe's team is guaranteed to make the best bread, and my father is guaranteed to take credit for the group's success. And while it is evidence of my immaturity, I'm irritated by Flip's good fortune.

My team has Carla, a tall, hunched, shy woman of perhaps thirty with a head only a few days past shaving. She seems perfectly nice, but flirting doesn't immediately come to mind. Next is Marcus, an attractive man in his thirties, Nordic, with a square jaw and carefully manicured fingernails and deck shoes and no socks who reminds me of the guys I met at fraternity parties in college. He is slightly too loud and slightly not funny.

And then there's Dave, who I've previously introduced. I am stunned to learn that Dave is not a seller of time-shares. He's a social worker. Personally, I would not want to have Dave as my social worker. Dave's hand is constantly in the air. When Hans or Catherine answers one of his questions, he nods gravely, as if he had the answer all along but posed the question for the benefit of the rest of us.

The remaining students make up Team Two. Gabriela is in her early thirties, solidly built with big brown eyes, long eyelashes, bleached hair, an accent that suggests she knows her Washington Heights from her Tribeca, and a pack of cigarettes in the pocket of her baker's jacket.

Marcel is tall, with brown eyes and a gray-streaked ponytail and a slight French accent. He has a permanent half-smile on his tanned face.

Lester is a slight, African American man with thick, frameless glasses. He seems to treat the class with extreme seriousness and has yet to smile as far as I have observed. He has a soft face and high cheekbones and full lips. He would make a convincing transvestite.

And finally, Michelle: less than five feet, Chinese American, bowl-cut hair. Flip would probably describe her as a "cookie." She says she used to be a bond trader and now she's looking to get into something a little less stressful.

Hans says bakers are more stressed than bond traders, get up earlier, work longer hours, and make a lot less money.

When we're done with the introductions, Hans enters the retarder and emerges with a plastic tub. He holds the container a few feet above the workbench and empties its contents onto the table. It lands with a satisfying splat. It is a slick, gelatinous mass of baguette dough, easily twenty pounds. This is dough that was mixed the day before and parked in the retarder for a slow initial rise.

Hans spends the next several minutes teaching us how to use a scale. I pay no attention. I'm consumed with the dough's slow but relentless movement toward the edge of the bench. Its advance is inexplicably compelling. I silently root for it to reach the rim and leap to ruin. But when it's an inch or two short of its target Hans scoops up the entire slab, folds it in two, and flips it over. Like a turtle in a terrarium, moseying repeatedly and ineffectually toward the glass, the dough once again makes for the perimeter of the bench. But the thrill is gone for me. I know what the dough can never know—that the German will never let it go.

Using a steel bench scraper Hans hacks into and then tears away a corner of the slab. He tosses it onto a digital scale. This process, unsurprisingly, is called *scaling*. The piece weighs 330 grams. The slab is something like 8,200 grams. Which means that without the benefit of any measuring tool Hans managed to cut off almost exactly 1/25th of the dough. I've never seen anything like it. It's as if he sees precise demarcations in the dough that are hidden from the rest of us. We applaud.

Next Hans demonstrates how to shape a baguette. He folds the hunk of dough in on itself while stretching it out a bit, to create a stubby, log-shaped mass, say three inches around and seven inches long. Then with the heels of his hands, starting from the center, he rolls outward, back and forth, to elongate the log. He ends up with a floppy, one-inch-thick, baguette-length cylinder. He shows us how, after this shaping, the dough settles into a second rise—called a final proof—on a linen cloth that has been folded into U-shaped compartments so the dough doesn't spread sideways.

Hans seems totally at one with the dough—there is no fight between them. When I made bread in California I thought of the dough as an enemy to be beaten, subdued, and then executed in the oven. Hans makes love to the dough with one hand while the other serves as a kind of conductor and, at critical moments, a facilitator.

He shapes a couple of baguettes and nestles them into the linen. So nestled the dough will rise for another hour before baking. Then he cuts off 330-gram hunks of dough and tosses them at us. I spread some flour in front of me on the bench. Hans appears out of nowhere, reaches in, and sweeps it onto the floor.

"You need only a little. Otherwise you'll kill the dough."

I let him step into my place at the bench. He takes a pinch of flour between his thumb and index finger and snaps his fingers while flicking his wrist, covering the table with a perfect dusting of flour—enough to prevent sticking, but not a molecule more than necessary.

I smash the dough into the table with the heels of my hands. It is resilient, not fragile. And once I move it around in my hands it doesn't feel sticky at all. I fold it over a few times, pry it off the bench with my yellow plastic bench scraper, and let it drop. If I were alone I'd hurl it at the ceiling to see if it would stick.

I try to follow the others, who look at me looking at them. I abort my first attempt at the dough log and try again. My second effort is close enough. I roll it out with the heels of my hands. I look over my baguette and think, *Not too shabby.* Then I glance around and see that mine is at least fifty percent too long.

But I am not alone. Gabriela has created something that looks more like a snake that has just consumed a guinea pig.

She is next to me. I tell her as much. She says, "Get outta hea," and smacks my arm with a flour-covered hand, releasing a cloud around us.

I try again on my baguette. Now I'm mad. Hans is across the room helping other students, so I slam the dough into the bench and beat it into submission. I like the way my knuckles leave an impression. Seems to me you have to treat the dough the way a dominatrix handles her clients. The dough must know who is in charge. The dough must accept from the start that it *will* submit. I hammer it with my fists and fling it around a few times before rolling it out. Gabriela takes a step away from me.

We deposit our first baguettes onto linen sheets and place the sheets in a plastic-sheathed cart that houses the loaves during their final proof. Then Hans wheels over a cart of ready-to-bake, fully proofed baguettes. The dough is fragile, almost impossible to handle. He shows us how to transfer the loaves to the oven in this flimsy final stage.

Starting at the end of a sheet of six loaves, he tips one raw baguette gently onto a wooden baker's peel. Then he rolls the dough from the peel onto a baguette loader, a machine that enables the baker to fill a bread oven with ten risen and shaped loaves at a time without ever touching the bread. The loader is essentially a portable conveyor belt. Once it's filled Hans uses a razor blade—also called a *lamé*—to score the tops of the loaves crosswise, about an inch deep. The slashes, which give French bread its distinctive ridges, permit the bread to release some of its interior water during baking. Hans then carries the loader to the ovens, slips it in, and pulls on a black plastic knob on the side of the machine. The loaves lay out onto the oven floor like toothpaste squeezes out onto a toothbrush. Hans closes the oven door and presses the steam injector button for three seconds.

We mill around for a while and then Hans pulls the finished loaves out of the oven and gathers us around the bench to inspect. He tears off the end of a baguette and passes the rest of the loaf around. We watch him inspect the bread. He holds it up to check its color. He bends it to test for elasticity. He sniffs the crumb and crust separately. And then he chomps off a piece and chews it, nodding with satisfaction.

We follow, each ripping off a chunk. The bread smells sweet and sour at the same time. It smells like grass and the skin of an orange, like fall leaves crumpled up in your hand. And unlike the cooled baguette I tried earlier, now it's crunchy. The hot crumb melts on my tongue.

"What do you think?" I ask Flip.

"Incredible," he says. "Just incredible."

My bad attitude about the artisanal baking class begins its retreat. I will almost certainly never understand baker's percentages or friction factors. But if I can come close to this—if I can produce something like these perfect tawny loaves of bubble-filled, butter-craving perfection, the week at FCI will have been worth every one of my father's pennies.

# chapter seven

# We Bake

TEAM ONE GATHERS by the white board to contemplate our first bordelaise. While I stare at the recipe and special instructions, Dave reads aloud from the board: "4,500 grams flour, unbleached and unbromated, 11.5 to 12% protein, minimum .50 ash content. 100 grams whole wheat, 400 grams rye. First rise overnight in the retarder, scaling, shaping, second rise in proofing baskets dusted with rice flour. Bake 15 minutes at 460 degrees and then 40 minutes at 400 degrees."

I understand all of this the way I understand the instructions in my car's owner's manual. I recognize the words. I even understand the general intent of the directions. But there's no way I'm actually going to try to change my spark plugs or oil. These directions seem similarly beyond my abilities. But the others appear undaunted, so I keep quiet.

To my surprise my teammates seem to know what they're doing. I follow them around the room as they gather the flour and other ingredients and then mix and knead them in the spiral mixer. I stand back, not wanting to be associated with what I assume will be a total disaster. Dave sends me off for a plastic bin. I pour a cup of oil into it so the finished dough doesn't stick during its first rise.

When the mixer shuts down and Marcus dumps the dough into the bin, I'm stunned to see that it looks perfect. It springs back when I stick my thumb into it. It's denser then the baguette dough we mixed earlier and has a richer, earthier smell. Though I've had only a little role in this process, I feel proud. Who needs Joe-the-pro?

As it happens, we do.

Moving on to our next assignment, Team One tackles its first load of ready-to-bake baguettes. All we have to do is transfer the delicate loaves to the baguette loader, score them, and slide them into the ovens. Dave leads off, pulling at the end of a linen cloth until a fully risen baguette rolls onto a peel. Then he tips the peel onto the loader and I'm up. I follow. It's a nerve-racking business because you can't adjust for mistakes by moving the dough around with your fingers. It's as delicate as a soap bubble floating in the air. If you touch it, it collapses.

When we finish filling two loaders Marcus insists that we huddle, place our flour-covered hands together, and give a cheer for Team One. Normally this is not my sort of thing, but I'm so pleased that we haven't totally fallen to pieces that I join in with gusto.

Dave and Carla leave Marcus and me to score the baguettes and load the oven while they gather ingredients for another batch of dough. We load brilliantly. Tragically, we forget to score. I blame Marcus, who rarely stops talking and says almost nothing. It's distracting, but I feel bad telling him to shut it because he's so freaking friendly. He wants to know what Flip and I are doing here, where I grew up, what he was like as a father. In the ten minutes we are alone together I learn more of his biographical details—lives in a small town in Vermont, sister works in one of those chain buffet restaurants, doesn't like women with small asses—than I know about people I've worked with for ten years.

So our baguettes go into the oven without the critical slashes that permit them to emit steam during baking.

We sheepishly bring this news to Hans, who says either our loaves will explode or they will not. Either way, he says, smiling, they will not be beautiful. He's correct. A few loaves detonate inside the oven. The ones that survive have the uncomfortably swollen, unnaturally firm look of fake boobs.

Our final task of the day is to prepare the liquid levain machine for tomorrow. The contraption, which Hans says goes for about twenty grand, consists of a large, stainless steel drum, kept at a constant, cool temperature by the refrigeration unit in which it is housed. A metal arm inside the drum ceaselessly churns a yeast-dense slurry. A spout on the outside of the machine allows the baker to siphon off a quart or two at a time for use in making various breads.

Each morning we pour a few cups of levain—preserved from the previous day, stored in a refrigerator overnight—into the empty levain machine. Then we add fresh flour and water and in a short time the yeast from the old levain mixes with the new fuel and begins to feed ravenously. At which point it can be used as the leavening agent in our bread recipes.

It is the levain, above all else, that makes this sort of baking different from what I've done at home. We use it to rise our breads, just like the freeze-dried yeast home bakers use. But the yeast in the liquid levain grows more strapping every time it feeds. It imbues the bread with subtle flavors that have developed over many years. In some French bakeries levain strains have been kept alive for more than a hundred years.

There's something implausible about the whole business. Every night someone takes a bit of this levain and walks it across the room to the refrigerator. And every morning someone feeds it and bakes with it and then preserves some for the next day. It seems impossible that in the thirty years since the school opened there hasn't been one uncaring, irresponsible person who, instead of rushing to rebuild the starter one morning, went to Jamaica.

Anyway I'm not going to be the one to kill FCI's levain, so I carefully follow Hans's instruction to preserve a few cups.

Then Dave and I focus on getting rid of the useless, end-of-the-day levain. Dave turns a knob and gallons of yeasty sludge spill into waiting buckets and onto the rubber mats lining the floor. We pour the levain into a nearby sink, returning with buckets of water, which we dump into the machine, thus diluting the sludge still inside. After several rounds of out-with-the-levain and in-with-the-water, all that is left to do is scrub the inside of the machine until it shines like a freshly minted nickel.

I'm still curious about the loaves that have been disappearing through the door near the ovens all day. So I ask Dave.

"They use them for the restaurant," he says, in a manner that suggests I am more than several french fries short of a Happy Meal. "Also they need them for the other classes, to make canapés and bread crumbs."

Dave is right. I am an idiot. Armpit deep in muck, blinded by my own sweat, for the first time I understand why we make so much bread. And where it all goes. And just how royally the French Culinary Institute is screwing us. We are *paying* for the privilege of staffing a for-profit bakery.

It's nearly four. We've been at it since eight. It's ninety degrees in the room and for much of the time we've been on our feet. My T-shirt is soaked through to my baker's gear. I'm ready to keel over. On our way back to the hotel after class I ask Flip, who has spent much of the past year strapped to a table and systematically poisoned, who is nearly twice my age, and who hasn't done any exercise since around the time of the Army-McCarthy hearings, how he's doing. He says, "Fine, superb."

I know my father is dying. I've spoken with doctors. I've seen X-rays. The thing is, though, he doesn't seem sick. He tires easily and his face has turned ruddy recently, as if he were a heavy drinker. But these symptoms seem less to do with the cancer than with the treatment. And even that hasn't taken the toll I'd expected. He remains among the hairiest people I've ever seen. And he may be alone in the annals of oncology for having reacted to chemotherapy with an increase in appetite and a considerable weight gain. It would not surprise me one bit if, several years from now, the experts declare him unkillable and refuse to have anything further to do with him.

It may be that these are among the last images I will have of my father—marching around the baking room, scraping hardened dough off a workbench, gnawing off chunks of a whole baguette with the side of his mouth. It's hard to fathom, though, because he looks fine. How am I supposed to come to terms with the idea of my father dying if my father refuses to look or act like he's dying? I'd rather not be in denial, but he's left me no alternative.

At six thirty we sit at a table in L'Ecole, the fancy restaurant staffed by FCI students. We are waiting for my father's oldest friend, Leon Arden, and his wife and daughter. The family lives in England, so Flip rarely sees them. Leon knows my dad is ill, but he doesn't know this is likely the last time they'll meet.

Flip is visibly nervous before dinner, rattling his fingers on the table, bouncing his skinny legs, clutching the stem of his martini glass as if it were the only oar in a life raft. I rub his back. He takes a deep breath, puffs out his cheeks, and forces all the air from his lungs. I tell him it's going to be all right. He nods.

My father is a loner. He lives far from his children. Though he has been married to my stepmother, Jane, for twenty-five years, they have never resided in the same house or the same state. And though he has friendly relations with many people, Flip says he has no real friends. Except for Leon.

Leon is a clever, witty, cheerful man around my dad's age, with slicked-back gray hair, chunky glasses that magnify his eyeballs, and a squeaky laugh. He is charming, a practiced conversationalist and drinker. Within a short time we are soused and chatting too loudly for the buttoned-down restaurant.

The waiter brings a basket filled with baguettes and bordelaise. Flip fingers a slice while he gives a long and, in critical respects, inaccurate address on artisanal bread making. Though we have been in the class for just one day, my father's tone is that of an expert baker on the witness stand. His know-it-all attitude irritates me. But I don't say so. Instead I make fun of the way he mispronounces lamé, the tool we use to score ready-to-bake loaves.

Leon shushes me. He must know that most of what Flip is saying is wrong, or at least that his professorial tone is ludicrous. But he listens raptly with an adoring look in his eyes and actually claps when my dad concludes. I have never seen someone love my father like this, an old friend, protective and loyal.

I envy it. Watching them bullshit and laugh and reminisce makes me yearn to let go of my anger. All right, so he wasn't around when I was seven, eleven, sixteen. That's history. I'm a grown-up now. Why can't I just love the guy, warts and all? I know he's going to die soon; so why can't I be more forgiving?

As we exit the restaurant my father holds Leon back for a few minutes. Leon's wife and daughter and I wait outside, under an awning, out of a hard, warm rain. When they emerge, Leon looks stunned. His jollity is gone. They do not make a fuss saying good-bye. They do it like they've always done, two buddies from way back, with a handshake and a slap on the shoulder. I hug Leon. I say I hope I'll be able to visit them in England. I hold out an umbrella and clutch Flip's arm while we slowly walk the few blocks back to our hotel.

# chapter eight

# Ingredients

IT IS SEVEN ON Friday morning, day two of the artisanal baking class. Flip has us off to FCI at least thirty minutes too early. And still, he seems to be in a rush. At our morning hangout, the D&D Deli, he's done with his bialy and ready to walk over to the school before my tea cools enough to drink.

I toss it when we go outside because I need the caffeine less than I need to avoid soaking through my clothes before we make it to FCI. I have not lived on the East Coast for a long time, so, unlike New Yorkers, who appear not to notice the weather, I resent the heat and humidity that makes me feel as if a hundred-pound Labrador retriever is licking my face all day long.

SoHo is busy with commuters. But my father is absolutely fearless. He thinks nothing of ignoring signals and stepping into oncoming traffic. Perhaps I should remind him that *I* am not terminally ill.

But I'm too exhausted to do anything other than follow. Sleep has been in short supply. I may never adjust to the weather. And the accommodations are comically inadequate. My father's snoring is indistinguishable from the sound of a bulldozer climbing a steep incline. And there's no way to sleep for more than an hour at a time on the couch. It's several inches shorter than me. The mattress on the pullout bed is so thin that I can feel the frame digging into my spine. Today I'm unable to rotate my neck more than a few degrees in either direction.

The air-conditioning continues to be a nightmare. My approach, which is hardly a solution, is to crank it up while we watch the evening news and then kill it when we turn in. By the morning I'm drenched in sweat, but I feel certain if I leave it on overnight I will get pneumonia. Flip doesn't seem to notice either way. He says he is, and appears to be, quite well rested.

When we reach the baking room it's empty. Flip takes a stool and spreads out the *Times* across the workbench. I watch him reading. His chin rests on his left thumb and he traces back and forth across his upper lip with his curled left index finger. This is how he has always looked while reading. I have a photo of him in his twenties, thin as a Number Two pencil, with thick, black-rimmed glasses, cigarette in his right hand, his head propped up in precisely this manner.

Every so often he blurts out a headline or a quote like, "Tom Ridge acknowledged today that the government's much-criticized color-coded terrorism alert system needs adjustment."

These outbursts are not designed to begin a dialogue. Even if I respond, as I do now, with "You can't be serious," he either ignores me or provides a few other details without really engaging.

Slowly shaking his head, he says, "Apparently they're going to come up with additional colors to warn us about regional threats."

"I don't see how anyone could object to more colors. I say the more colors the better."

He doesn't reply.

I page through our instruction and recipe book, which contains a summary history of bread making.

"Did you know the people who stormed the Bastille before the French Revolution were looking for wheat?"

This breaks his concentration, as I knew it would.

"I'm a historian, remember? I get paid to know that."

Which does not, you will notice, actually answer my question.

He goes back to the paper.

Flip and I banter. This is how we avoid talking. After we see one another for one of our two- or three-day visits, I feel as if I have been to a birthday party, drunk too much Coke, eaten several slices of birthday cake but no pizza. I feel full, slightly nauseated, but still hungry.

I've tried to talk to my dad about my feelings, about our history. But we don't often get very far before we swing back into chitchat. I rarely press him, because I'm not really sure I want to know the truth; because I worry that pushing him too hard might lead him to disappear as he disappeared when I was five; and because if I open my leaky bag of anger and disappointment, maybe I'll never get it closed again.

"So what made you want to take this class, anyway?"

Without looking up he says, "I wanted to learn to make bread. Why else would I be here?"

"It just seems a little weird, out of nowhere, to decide to start baking. You always have crappy bread at your house."

"It's Clemson, what do you want?"

Other than excellent barbecue, Clemson is not known for its cuisine.

I turn to a section of our manual called "Function of Ingredients."

Wheat flour, I read, is the essential building block of bread. It contains proteins called gliaden and glutenin. When flour is mixed with water, these proteins form gluten, a cohesive three-dimensional structure that captures gases, like the carbon dioxide produced by yeast, and permits dough to rise while remaining resilient and cohesive.

"Did you ever make bread at home?" I ask.

He gives up and puts away the paper.

"I tried to make bagels once. They came out like rocks."

"What about when you were a kid?" I say.

"Not in my family. Maybe other people did."

I reach below the bench, into a bin, and pull out a handful of Sir Lancelot flour. I practice the flick-of-the-wrist, snap-of-the-fingers dusting technique Hans demonstrated yesterday.

"So why did you want to take this class with *me* anyway?"

"I thought it would be fun."

"You could have asked Guthrie." My younger brother.

"He couldn't take the time off. Plus he's got the kids."

"What about Cullen?"

"Nancy can't eat bread." Nancy is Cullen's wife. She is allergic to gluten.

"Did you actually ask either of them?"

"No. What is this?"

"What about Wendy?"

Wendy, my younger sister, is a doctor in New York. We haven't spoken in several years.

"She's busy."

"And I'm not busy?" We sit in silence for a few moments. Then I say, "It'll be interesting to see how it goes when you really get sick. Then we'll *have* to be around one another."

He raises his eyebrows. "You think *so*, huh?"

I shrug. "No?"

"The only time you'll be around each other is when I'm gone, and at that point it won't be my problem. I already told Guthrie and Cullen, I don't want them coming to Clemson."

"What if you can't take care of yourself?"

"I'll probably die of a heart attack."

"But if not then we'll want to come down, so we'll be together. One big happy family."

"I told Guthrie, the only one I want around would be you." Me? "Because you're handling it well." I am? "And because you don't have kids."

"I have dogs."

"It's not the same. Plus we can bake bread."

"Not in *your* crappy oven."

"I'll buy a new one," Flip says, unfurling the *Times* for another try.

"Do me a favor," I say. "Try not to squander my meager inheritance."

Water, the second key building block of a loaf of bread, serves three purposes. First, it hydrates the gliadin and glutenin proteins to form the gluten molecules. Second, it acts as a solvent and dispersing agent for other ingredients such as salt, sugar, and milk. And finally, it assists with the gelatinization process during baking when—at temperatures of 140 to 180 degrees Fahrenheit—starches in the flour rupture, increasing the surface area of the dough and releasing water into the available spaces, thus transforming visco-elastic dough into the more rigid baked product state.

In the next few minutes our classmates wander in, which I suppose comes as a relief to Flip. He turns to Gabriela and asks about her plan to take over a bakery close to the school. She says she's lived her whole life in Little Italy. Joe, Flip's teammate, is her baker. She's in the class to learn the nuts and bolts of the business. And she's brought along Joe to expand his repertoire beyond Italian bread and cookies.

Flip leans into the bench and clasps his hands together. I recognize the pose. He's going into story mode. The hands will come apart for emphasis, float down to the table for a rest, and then come together again. He'll remove his glasses when something he says gets a big laugh. He'll rub his eyes, pause for effect, and then return the glasses to his face. Although the story is intended for the group, he'll look only at one person, in this case Gabriela.

In the late fifties, Flip begins, he lived with his wife in a fourth-floor walk-up on Mott Street, in the heart of Little Italy. The first month no one talked to them. The men made lewd remarks to Cookie. Flip felt silly for not having anticipated that a Jewish couple might not immediately fit into the neighborhood. They knew some of the men on the street must be in the Mafia. Friends were nervous to visit. They thought about leaving.

My classmates fall for him. I look around and see that they are hanging on his every word. He describes how the Mott Street guys were dressed—gray slacks and long coats over undershirts. He says the floors in their two-room apartment sagged so badly he was convinced they'd end up in the apartment below if they ran the bath. His portrait of the naïve couple is funny and even suspenseful—what would become of the newlyweds? Would they get chased out of town?

After a couple of months, Flip says, their neighbors started waving and the same men who had whistled at my mother now helped her carry groceries up to the apartment. A few months later Cookie couldn't get her car out of a parking space. A few tough-looking locals picked the car up and carried it into the street. Flip says it turned out to be the safest, friendliest place they ever lived.

For the first time in my life I am with my father while he tells a group of strangers about his life. It's maddening. He describes this history, my history, casually, as an entertainment for our classmates. Here, now, I can't possibly ask the questions that come to mind: What was Cookie like then? Were you in love? Was she depressed? Did you fight? Did you regret marrying her? Did you talk about having children? Did it ever occur to you that this person might not be a very good mother, or that you might eventually tire of your family and leave?

He doesn't seem to care how the story might make me feel. I have an urge to wave my hand in front of his face and say, "Hey Pop, remember me?"

Chef Hans enters the room. The chatting ceases. He walks to the head of the table, places his hands on the bench, and leans on his muscular arms. He stares at the table for a few moments and then points behind him to the white board with the team assignments for the day.

"Well," he says, the light German accent turning the *W* into a slurred *V*, "I think it's time to bake."

We scurry to the board with our notepads. Team One huddles. We're missing Marcus. But we can't wait for him if we have any hope of completing our baking chores before lunch. Our first task is a baguette recipe made with *pate fermentee*. It looks a lot like a straight dough recipe—5,000 grams flour, 3,100 grams water, 100 grams salt, and 50 grams of fresh cake yeast. But to add flavor, texture, and body to the bread, we'll mix in a large hunk of raw dough—called the *mere* or *mother*—from a prior batch of baguettes.

*Pate fermentee* is one of the four so-called *preferment* methods commonly used in French baking. Artisans long ago discovered that if you add a previously fermented, flour-water concoction to a straight dough recipe you get hardier, tastier bread. So, along with the old-dough method, bakers spice things up with *sponge* (a relatively dry, fermented flour-water mixture), *poolish* (a wetter version of sponge), or *biga* (varies, but typically is like the *pate fermentee,* but the dough is preserved before the addition of salt).

Dave jumps into the driver's seat, ordering me off for water and yeast. He and Carla take care of the flour, salt, and *pate.* When I return to the mixer with my scaled ingredients, Dave stands at attention. He checks off his list as we load up. Two minutes at low speed and then another two at high. Oil a tub. Dump the machine-mixed and kneaded sludge for a long first fermentation in the retarder. Then, with Dave at the helm, we're off to scale out and shape a batch of baguette dough that went into the retarder yesterday.

Yeast leavens. It consumes sugars and releases carbon dioxide as a by-product. The gas fills the three-dimensional gluten structures and the dough rises. Without yeast, bread would be as dense and difficult to chew as brick. Yeast, as it ferments, also produces alcohol, acids, and heat. These condition the flour and contribute to flavor development in the final product. Bakers yeast (*Saccharomyces cerevisiae*) is available in both a freeze-dried version, which is what you find in grocery stores, and a fresh form, which is called cake-yeast and comes in blocks the size of bricks.

There are many other ingredients that artisanal bakers regularly use—salt, sugar, shortening, milk, mold inhibitors, wheat gluten, diastatic malt, fungal amylases, protease enzymes, oxidizing agents, calcium peroxide, dough strengtheners, crumb softeners. But all you really need to make bread is flour and water and yeast.

Our missing teammate, Marcus, joins us more than an hour after class begins. He says he was at a bar until five in the morning. His hair is disheveled and I can still smell alcohol on his breath. He asks me what he can do to help. I tell him he should ask Dave.

A short time later I see Abby slip out the door of the baking room and I follow. I notice that she is wearing dark sunglasses. I catch up to her.

"Pretty bright in here," I say.

She looks around furtively.

"I'm in disguise. The bursar is after me."

She explains she has yet to pay her outstanding fees. I have the sense that affordability is not the issue. She likes being on the run.

"Are you leaving permanently?" I say.

"I need coffee. But the bursar's been lurking for me in the main stairwell. I'm trying to find an alternate exit."

I follow, without being invited. We escape down the back stairs and find our way to a nearby coffee cart.

"You and your dad are quite a team," she says.

"What's that supposed to mean?"

"You have fun together."

"We're more like an army than a team. He's a general and I'm a draftee."

"You seem to get along well."

I raise my eyebrows and grunt.

"Well, I think he's charming and hilarious," she says.

And he is. Everyone likes Flip.

"You mean like Ted Bundy hilarious?" I say.

"What?" She heard me.

"No, it's true. He's a wonderful guy."

# chapter nine

# We Talk

S HORTLY BEFORE LUNCH all twelve students swarm two loads of baguette dough and a batch of bordelaise. We are like ants that have discovered a bunch of bananas recently run over by an 18-wheeler. Hans and Catherine stand back like nervous parents while we assemble around a workbench, shoulder-to-shoulder, ready with our scrapers and small piles of flour for dusting.

Tall Marcel and small Michelle lop off chunks of dough from a huge slab for scaling. Marcel's scale indicates his piece is underweight so he piles on tiny scraps of dough until he has enough for a loaf. The scalers slide lumps of dough down the table and we pass it along as in a bucket brigade. After shaping our loaves we push them into the middle of the bench where Lester organizes neat rows. And then we signal for another future baguette. In fifteen minutes we whack through twenty-five kilos of raw dough.

It occurs to me that I've been sucked into one of those team building exercises I've been avoiding my whole life. I'm already becoming attached to these people. I'm proud of our work together. We spread out the shaping practice evenly among us. We shout encouragements across the bench. No one hogs scaling time. No one criticizes Marcel because his scaling is too slow. No one tells me my bordelaise are lopsided.

Also, I'm beginning to see the logic of our enslavement to the bread needs of L'Ecole. Because we have to pump so much bread out of the kitchen every day, we end up mixing and scaling and shaping and proofing and scoring and baking until those processes become routine. The first day I sweated and cursed through every loaf. Now, while we work, Gabriela and Marcus argue about whether *School of Rock* was a better movie than *Seabiscuit*, Flip chats with Laurie about his occasional work lecturing on cruise ships, and I think about my dogs and where Flip and I will eat tonight.

A day and a half into the class, we're becoming bakers.

Twenty minutes later, lunch: house-made bratwurst and sauerkraut, spinach salad with pieces of blue cheese the size of a golf ball, and garlic mashed potatoes. And, of course, slices of olive-oil-brushed, grilled bordelaise, care of the June 2003 FCI Artisanal Baking class.

"How's the sausage?" I say.

"Excellent. Truly outstanding." Flip's head is bent over his plate. His baker's hat doesn't budge. He shovels food into his mouth. "You're not eating?"

The full-time culinary students prepare lunch. Given how little I've slept, it might well put me into a coma.

We're sitting off in a corner of the room, stools pulled up to a metal counter. Some of our classmates eat at the benches. Others have disappeared into SoHo for the hour.

I say, "I figured out I must have been conceived right after the Kennedy assassination."

He raises his head for a moment.

"Really?"

"You don't remember that?" I say.

"No," he says, and turns back to his plate.

"I think that could explain why I'm such a nervous person. There must have been a lot of anxiety in the air at the time."

"I never liked Kennedy," he says, several strands of caramelized onion hanging from his lower lip. "He got us into Vietnam."

"Come on. Think back. You were upset. You and Mom clung to each other through those dark autumn days. Nine months later, I arrived."

He laughs.

"How can you not eat after this morning?" he says. "I'm starving."

"Quit changing the subject."

"I'm not changing the subject," he says. "I'm telling you I didn't have much use for Kennedy and neither did your mother. We'd been trying to have a baby for a long time. Your mom had three miscarriages between Cullen and you."

"So I was truly a labor of love."

"Yes."

I snatch his last bite of bratwurst.

"Why don't you get your own?"

"Yours is fine. So if you wanted me so much why weren't you there when I arrived?"

His mouth is full of sausage and potatoes. He holds up his right index finger while he chews.

"Why are you asking me this?"

"It just seems weird that you wouldn't want to be around when your wife gave birth."

"When we were in Charlottesville I wrote a book about a gang of mobsters on the run from the law. They decide to hide out at a summer camp, posing as counselors. It was called *Don't Tinkle on the Gangsters*."

"And this explains why you were a thousand miles away the night I was born."

"You want to know what happened or you want to talk?"

An agent at William Morris told Flip the book was terrible but his dialogue was good and advised him to try writing plays. Flip signed up to audit a class on playwriting at the University of Virginia. On the first day of class the professor described the elements of a play. That took about ten minutes. He told the students that by the end of the term they should all have completed one dramatic work. Then he wished the students good luck and left the room.

A week later my father walked into the professor's office with a first act. The professor looked at him as if he was out of his mind, told him he was working too quickly, that the play must be dreadful, and sent him away. A week later my dad returned with a completed three-act comedy. The professor read it, thought it was funny, and told Flip he didn't need the class. He advised him to send it off to New York.

Flip made a list of theatrical agents. He sent it to one named Bertha Klausner on a Tuesday. The following Monday morning she called my father in Virginia to tell him she'd sold it.

"So, now, tell me," I say. "What part of that story is true?"

"All of it," he says. He is indignant.

My father is a liar. He is not the sort who lies for personal gain. He doesn't falsify his taxes or cheat on my stepmother, Jane. But still, he's a totally unreliable reporter. Sometimes he fills in the blanks, as I'm certain he is doing with at least a few of the details regarding the sale of his play. Also, he pretends to be an expert when he is not. And very often he exaggerates and hyperbolizes to spice up a story. It probably took him more than a week to finish the first act of his play. But to the uninitiated, oblivious that most of the particulars are made up, details like these can be quite compelling.

So why should I care? It's a good story. What difference could it possibly make whether it's true or partially true or complete nonsense?

"You're telling me you remember the day of the week Bertha called you. From, what, more than forty years ago."

"I remember it perfectly," Flip says. "You want me to go on?"

The thing is, I have a stake in the truth. I would like to get some of this history—my history—straight. I'd like to meet and perhaps even get to know the real Flip Schaffer, if such a person exists. It's not that he's always lying; it's just impossible to know one way or another. He's been telling these stories for so many years I wonder whether he even knows which are remembered and which concocted. Time is running out. I'd feel less like batting him on the head with a baker's peel if he'd at least make an effort.

"Fine," I say. "Just do me a favor and give me a signal when you start to veer off into the land of the totally made up."

The play was called *One in a Row*. The main character was a failed literary agent in New York. The agent's business is in disarray, on the verge of total collapse, when one of his clients, a young, idealistic writer, publishes a hit. The agent is suddenly thrust into the limelight, taking meetings with Hollywood directors, having lunch with big-shot publishers.

Then the author decides he's through with writing and informs the agent that he's off to the Peace Corps. And the agent spends the rest of the play trying to get his client to write a second book.

"I've always thought that was a great title," I say.

"Titles I can do. But the play had no ending. That was the problem."

I've heard the story of *One in a Row* many times before. It is part of the Flip Schaffer legend, that he wrote a terrific play, that it was headed for Broadway, that all he lacked was an ending. With an ending he could have been as successful as Neil Simon.

"How did it end?"

"I don't remember. I just know it was bad."

"How can you not remember?"

"It's forty years."

"But you remember the day of the week Bertha called."

"Yes."

He can't possibly remember what he claims to, and he can't possibly have forgotten the ending of his play. It's maddening. But he won't budge.

For a while, Flip says, Jackie Mason was interested in playing the agent. *True, not true? Who knows?* He met with Mason at the Stage Delicatessen in New York. The star told him he liked the play, but ultimately decided he didn't have the time to get involved. Mason asked my father what he did to earn a living. Flip told him he was a professor of history. Mason said, "Don't quit your day job."

Flip sold the play in 1962, but it wasn't until the spring of 1964, after he and Cookie and my older brother, Cullen, moved to Michigan, that the producers found a director and put together a cast. The play would open in summer stock, at the Town and Country Playhouse in Rochester, New York, on August 12, 1964. My birthday.

Flip says Cookie's due date was shortly after the premiere date. There was nothing they could do to change the opening. It had been set for months. They discussed it and agreed he should go. He returned to Michigan before Cookie got out of the hospital.

"It's not like I didn't want to be there," Flip says. "I just couldn't be."

The star of *One in a Row* was a well-regarded comedian named Phil Foster. On opening night in Rochester, with critics and potential investors in the audience, Foster ad-libbed his final speech, changing the ending dramatically.

"You must have been unhappy," I say.

"I was ready to tear the man's throat out. But my ending was no better than Foster's."

"The ending you don't remember."

"Right."

"Maybe I'll be able to figure it out," I say.

"Nah. I threw all of it away years ago."

I have asked to see my father's writing many times over the years. He's always said the same thing: "When I'm gone, it's yours."

My face gets hot and my chest feels like I've just sprinted up two flights.

"You threw what out?" I say.

"Everything. I couldn't stand to look at it. It was all such crap."

If he's telling the truth, I'm furious. But is he?

"Do you not remember saying you'd leave the plays to me? Do you not remember *promising* to save them for me?"

Chef Hans claps his hands to start the afternoon session. Flip slips off his stool and rushes to join his team.

Hans leads us through our first handmade bread, a lavash, which is a thin, leavened, skillet-grilled flatbread. Unlike the machine-mixed-and-kneaded baguettes and bordelaise, which call for kilos of ingredients at a time, this is a home-sized recipe. Flip turns to me and gives me the thumbs-up. In other words, finally something we can tackle without a hundred grand in kitchen gear. I glare at him and give him the thumbs-down. If we were alone I'd flash another finger altogether.

Chef Catherine jots the ingredients on the white board. We scribble in our notebooks and then scatter. When we work as teams there are plenty of resources to go around. But now we're on our own so there's a crunch for scales, flour, honey, yeast, salt, water.

For the first time Flip is on his own, unable to rely on his teammates for support and guidance. I watch with amusement, and then horror, as he falls completely to pieces. The competition for ingredients turns him into a cranky four-year-old. He grumbles that for this kind of money they could have a few more scales. Halfway across the room with his yeast, which he carries on a sheet of butcher paper, he dumps it on the floor and has to start over. He's the last to settle at his workspace and by that time beads of sweat cover his reddened faced.

Hans instructs us to sweep the flour into an inch-high, inch-wide ring. With my left hand I pour water, yeast, and honey into the middle of the ring. With my right hand I combine small quantities of flour with the other ingredients. At first it turns into a sloppy mush. But after ten minutes of mixing and kneading I have a smooth, springy, sweet-smelling lavash dough. After a rise I'll divide it in three, roll it out with a pin, and grill it in a cast-iron pan.

I turn to look at my dad's progress. His earlier frustration now seems mild by comparison. Flip's dough is a mess and he's throwing a tantrum worthy of any preschooler. If you poured five tablespoons of water on a pound of animal crackers, and stomped on it a few times, you'd have something that looks a lot like his lavash. I can tell he's furious, at the dough, at Hans, at himself for wasting his precious time in this stupid class with this stupid, impossible lavash.

Flip also has ignored Hans's instruction to keep his left hand out of the mix, in order to be able to add ingredients as needed. Both his hands are caked with sticky muck, bits of which have affixed themselves to his mustache and glasses. I don't dare let him catch me looking, so I shift positions and surveil him out of the corner of my eye.

No matter how hard he works the dough, it doesn't loosen up. It clings to his hands so that every time he raises them above the bench the entire mess of dough comes with them. He slams the dough onto the table, over and over again, with increasing violence. Nervous that he may be alarming his teammates working nearby, I walk over to assist.

He looks rabid. "I don't know what the hell's wrong with me. I just can't do it."

I glance at his notes and see that he's mistakenly written *20 grams water*. The recipe calls for 200 grams, which explains the parched look of his dough.

"I think you might need more water," I say.

"I don't know what the hell I need," he snaps back.

I back away and return to my spot across the room. I wave Catherine over and, keeping my voice down, I ask her to intervene.

Flip never hit me. But as a child he terrified me. This is because sometimes he became so enraged he seemed as if he could hardly keep himself from wringing my throat. His anger did not seem containable.

He also scared me because I was never sure what was going to put him over the edge. Sometimes I made too much noise or forgot to take out the garbage, and he scolded me but he didn't lose it. Sometimes I left the television on or misplaced a key and his face turned red and the veins pulsed out of his neck. He yelled so loud I wanted to plug my ears with my fingers, but I didn't dare. My stomach tumbled with shame.

When I was nine he took two friends and me ice-skating. Flip couldn't skate, so he leaned over the side of the railing smoking, waving when I zipped past. A couple of times he motioned for me to slow down. I collided with a group of younger girls. We slid across the ice, but no one was hurt. Flip screamed at me from the railing, his voice ricocheting around the rink and drawing the attention of hundreds of kids and parents. He pointed to the bleachers behind him and yelled, "Dylan, get out here. Get! Out!"

When I reached the edge of the rink he stuck his cigarette in his mouth, pressing down with his lips until the glowing end stuck almost straight up, grabbed me by the elbow, and dragged me off the ice. He pressed so hard on my arm I thought it was going to break. I doubt he was really pressing that hard, but I remember worrying for my arm, and even worrying about what would happen to Flip if he did break it.

Mostly I think Flip scared me as a kid because I figured if I made him mad enough he would just disappear.

chapter ten

# That Evening

"MOM ALWAYS SAID the reason you moved out was because you wanted to write." We're on our way to dinner. I'm in a sour mood and I don't try to hide it. "That you wanted to be free of the kids."

"Completely bogus. Completely wrong, like so much of what your mother said."

"People have left their families for less," I say.

He walks headlong into traffic and I swing my arm into his chest, thus probably saving his life. He does not thank me.

"It's nonsense," he says. "I wrote plenty with the kids around. If I showed you my collected works, you'd be amazed. I'm stunned sometimes how much I wrote."

It's six thirty. The sun, finally thinking about setting, sneaks over the top of buildings on Broadway. I'm recently showered and dressed in shorts and sandals, so the heat is less bothersome. Flip, who is always anxious to get wherever Flip is heading, particularly if it involves eating, is anxious to get to dinner. But I dally at every curbside display of sunglasses and books. I try on ten pairs of shades. He folds his arms and points to his watch. I tell him to go on if he likes. But he waits.

"I'd be thrilled to see your collected works," I say. "But you claim to have none of it."

"I moved so many times. It got lost."

I stare at him for ten seconds without speaking.

"Am I losing my mind or did you tell me just a few hours ago that you threw it away?"

"I threw it away."

"But three seconds ago you said you lost it."

"I threw it away."

I have a fake Rolex in my hand. I would like to place it on the pavement and stomp on it. I should do it and Flip should have to pay for it. I put it back on the table.

"But I'm not insane, right? Moments ago, you said you lost it."

"I said, 'It got lost.' "

"I assume you know that losing something and throwing it away are different."

"I'm getting tired of being cross-examined."

"This is very important to me, Dad. You saved nothing. The truth."

"It's the truth. It would be different if I'd been successful, but I failed. I wanted to be a writer and I didn't make it."

Flip says that on the night *One in a Row* opened in Rochester, hours before I was born, a famous producer approached him. He put his arm around Flip's shoulder and shook his hand. I imagine the guy was chomping on an unlit cigar at the time. The producer said, "Son, you have ninety-five percent of a Broadway hit here." Then he dropped Flip's hand and said, "Nobody wants ninety-five percent."

Flip continues: "You could say, look, for a guy with a Ph.D. in history, writing ninety-five percent of a hit his first time out isn't too bad."

"You could."

"Why should I have saved any of it? I don't want to be reminded of what might have been. To save stuff you have to think it's somehow important. I never had that kind of ego."

He says the last sentence with an entirely straight face, which is an achievement on the order of the pyramids. I could spend the rest of the evening riffing off this single assertion, but mostly I just want to figure out what happened to the plays. Flip is totally unreliable, but I always assumed there would be some kind of truth in his stories; that I might get to know him through his fiction.

"You still had the plays when you were living in the Bronx. I remember trying to look at one. You got angry and grabbed it out of my hand. I couldn't have been more than eight or nine. You said, and I quote: 'I will leave them to you in my will.' Did you forget that?"

"I'm sorry, Sonny."

"Me, too."

We eat in SoHo, at a diner pretending to be a restaurant. They get $4.50 for lemonade. Cullen, Nancy, their nine-year-old, Anschel, and Nancy's parents join us. I'm glad to have the company because after two days in class with Flip, right on time, I'm feeling a riptide of impatience and annoyance tugging at me. The wrong thing to do is to swim against the current, but this is precisely my instinct.

At the restaurant with the rest of the family, Flip orders soft-shell crabs. Given the opportunity, this is what my father always orders. We wait too long for our food. We eat. The others ask Flip and me about the class. He's quiet, which is rare. I ask him if he's all right and he nods, taking a long swig from his vodka martini. I lean over and promise, quietly, that I won't tell anyone about his lavash. He smiles. But I continue to watch him and something is definitely up. He hacks at his crab like it's ivy. He drops his fork on his plate carelessly. And then I get it.

"How's the food?" I say. He turns so his left ear, the size of a dessert plate, faces me. And he cups it with his hand to enhance his hearing. I try again. "How's the crab?"

"It's crap."

There's a joke here, but he says this in a manner that strongly suggests there is no room for levity.

"You managed to eat most of it."

"I was famished. What was I supposed to do?"

The others pay attention now because he's stiffened in his seat and raised his voice.

"What's wrong with it?" I say.

"I don't know where they got this chef. The man is a complete idiot. He takes a perfectly decent soft-shell crab and *encrusts* it with polenta. It's just stupid. There's absolutely no reason to *encrust* it. I don't know who he's trying to impress."

This is not idle postmeal debriefing. Flip takes the *encrusting* personally. He is furious, calling the chef names because he didn't like his dinner. The man is a churl. He somehow thinks he can say anything at any time, no matter how asinine.

"You know what, Dad? You don't call someone an *idiot* because you disagree with his cooking style," I say, not attempting to hide my disdain. "It's not only obnoxious, it's *incorrect* to say the chef is *stupid* because he puts polenta on crab. That seems more of an aesthetic choice than a measure of his intellect."

"It's just beyond me why anyone would ruin good crab like this."

"Wonder all you want, but don't call another human being an idiot because you didn't like your dinner."

Flip does not respond. He does not take well to being chastised and has a familiar look on his face: it says, I don't need this aggravation; I don't need children or bad cooks or hard questions from my son about my life; just leave me alone.

I take a sip of water. The waiter returns to the table to clear plates and ask about dessert. We pass and wait in near silence for the check.

Spending a week with my father was a bad idea. I see now that I came to New York with unrealistic expectations. I hoped he would make some attempt to resolve things with me. But he won't or maybe just can't talk to me about the things that matter.

I don't know what I was thinking. This is a seventy-two-year-old man who, in the company of his closest family members, loved ones he will likely be leaving for good in weeks or months, throws a tantrum over crab.

Outside the restaurant I say my good-byes and tell Flip I'll meet him back at the hotel.

It's a balmy Friday night and SoHo is packed. Lines of would-be diners stream out of tiny restaurants, smoking, gabbing, drinking red wine from paper cups. Paunchy men in baseball caps and athletic shorts that hang below the knee and white muscle shirts sit on benches by a small park. I walk too quickly, weaving through strollers and lovers and gangs of teenagers. I listen to rap music on my iPod. Everyone seems to have a partner tonight and I'm alone.

Up the block I watch people emerging from a storefront with bowls of what seems to be ice cream. When I walk closer I see the place is called Rice to Riches. I assume it serves ice cream made of rice milk. The place is jammed so I figure I should try it. For ten minutes I wait my turn, scanning the flavors. Although there are many exotic varieties, I decide to stick with chocolate. I place my order and pay six dollars for a "solo." This seems pretty steep, but I suppose the rent must be insane on this street. Plus, the store is significantly more stylish than the unadorned, Baskin-Robbiny places I'm used to. It's decorated like the Jetsons' apartment.

The counter person hands me a dish with a plastic cover on it so I don't actually see what's in it until I leave the store. Which is when I discover that I've just paid six bucks not for a scoop of rice-milk ice cream, but for a bowl of not-even-very-cold, mushy rice mixed with chocolate sauce. It's a rice pudding store. I had no idea such a thing existed.

Feeling duped, I stand in the middle of the sidewalk paralyzed by a mix of disappointment, embarrassment, and pique. I stare at the attractive but unsmiling woman with no hair who served me my rice pudding, deciding if I should go in and say something. And then I see that it's my own fault. Had I not been so excited by the thought of eating ice cream on a warm New York night to make myself feel better about my rotten luck at having such a flawed father, I would likely have noticed the many clues that I'd soon be paying six dollars for a bowl of rice mush, including the perhaps fifty people eating rice mush around me, and the many references to rice pudding on the menu, and the complete absence of ice cream or its close relatives in the store.

There is only one person in the world who will feel *exactly* the way I do about Rice to Riches, who will agree that bowls of six-dollar rice pudding are an abomination, an offense against dessert. There is only one man who will share my desire to stand outside Rice to Riches with a sign that reads I SCREAM, YOU SCREAM, WE ALL SCREAM FOR . . . RICE PUDDING?

I rush back to the hotel. Flip has left the door ajar because we have only one key. Every light in the suite is on. He is passed out on his bed.

I turn on the television and watch the ten o'clock news. An editor at the *New York Times* has resigned because one of his writers filed a series of bogus reports. The story about the fake reporting has been all over the news in the past couple of weeks, and in my opinion it's much ado about nothing. The world is not so slowly disintegrating and all the solemn hand wringing over a few made up facts seems entirely beside the point.

I say, out loud, to the TV, about the editor who quit, "The man's a complete idiot."

And then I laugh, and say, out loud, *"I'm so screwed."*

Because it's seems certain that one day I will be seventy-two and I will throw a fit over rice pudding or encrusted soft-shelled crab. Jen will scold me. And I will sulk.

She'll say, "You're out of your mind."

And she'll be right.

# chapter eleven

# The Weekend

SUNDAY MORNING I HOPE to sleep until noon, to cut into the hefty sleep debt I've amassed over the first few nights in New York. I'm on the couch. When Flip emerges from the bedroom, at seven thirty a.m., we trade places. I hug him and tell him I'm going back to sleep. I close the door behind me and crumple onto his bed. My nose is in his pillow. It smells of Flip—unbrushed teeth, coffee, and body odor that if it were not my father's might be noxious.

It reminds me of being four, with orders from my mother to wake him. I'd climb into bed and lie with my nose just inches from his, feeling his breath on my face.

"Daddy," I'd say, whispering at first. Flip was almost impossible to wake. As I got louder, he'd eventually stir.

He'd pop up like one of those spring-loaded Halloween corpses out of a coffin, and mumble, "Whaaaat? What's wrong?"

"Mom says you have to get up."

In the time it took me to finish the sentence, Flip would have conked out.

I'd climb on top of him and put my lips half a foot from his ear.

"Daddy," I'd shout.

"Whaaaat? What's wrong?"

And so on.

Back in the present, I'm startled awake by a high-pitched, metallic whine that seems to be coming from outside the bedroom door. I look at my watch. I've been back asleep for eighteen minutes. First I think it's the air conditioner in its death throe. But once I'm fully awake I hear that it's an instrument of some kind. There must be a six-year-old next door with his first recorder. I pull on some boxers and a T-shirt and prepare to storm the kid's room and punch him out.

It's Flip. Although he has end-stage lung cancer my father has taken up a wind instrument—the tin whistle.

"You must be kidding me," I say, standing in the doorway.

He ignores me and continues playing, following along in a book. He hits one in four notes. I gather he is attempting to play "London Bridge."

When he reaches the end of the page he looks up.

I say nothing, but spread my arms apart and raise my eyebrows in an effort to convey, *Can you fill me in here?* without actually saying it, because if I say it, it will almost certainly come out sounding like, *What the fuck are you doing?*

"Did I wake you?" he says.

"Yes."

"Sorry, Sonny. You want me to stop?"

There's no way I'll be able to fall back asleep.

"Let me try it," I say.

It's a cheap, gold-colored tin whistle with a neon yellow tip. I sound as bad as Flip. I return it.

"By all means, play. I wasn't really sleeping."

He takes the whistle for another spin, with similar results.

"I'm getting pretty good, huh?" he says.

No, in fact, you're not even pretty bad.

"Yeah."

He stows the tin whistle in his fanny pack before we leave for the day. When he's in the bathroom, I remove it. I do not toss it out the window, a restraint for which I believe I am entitled to a medal of some kind.

When Flip emerges we exit the hotel, walk east up Rivington, and then south on Chrystie. At a light I turn around and see more familiar parts of Manhattan—the Chrysler building, the Empire State—in the distance. It is already very warm and the sky is an opaque blue.

We walk. Flip talks.

Unlike many Jews who grew up in New York in the first half of the twentieth century, my father was not from the Lower East Side. He was born October 29, 1930, in the Bronx. His father, Louis, had been part of the mass Jewish migration from Europe to the United States in the early 1900s. In 1935 Louis, apparently pining for the sort of hostile environment to which he'd become accustomed in the old country, moved the family to the Yorkville neighborhood of Manhattan, an area settled predominantly by non-Jewish immigrants.

There he opened a small clothing store. The family relocated several times, but always within a few blocks of my grandfather's business. Flip's mother became an invalid after the move from the Bronx. The family's apartment developed a stale, forlorn air, so after school Flip roamed the city with his friends, west to the Metropolitan Museum and Central Park, east to the river. As an adolescent he commuted forty minutes by subway to high school on the Lower East Side.

When they were old enough to contribute to the family business, Flip and his older brother, Frank, stood on the sidewalk outside my grandfather's store to make sure no one stole from boxes of merchandise out front. Louis said that if a woman asked for a pair of large stockings, and they had none, they should stretch out a smaller pair with their hands and insist that the hose would fit the customer.

Louis said that if the store caught fire they should not call the police or the fire department. Insurance would cover the losses. If the authorities came, Louis told his sons, they would steal everything.

Once Flip heard someone outside the store call his father a Jew bastard. Louis, who was five feet tall, knocked the man halfway across the street. Flip and his friends heard Joe McWilliams, an anti-Semitic rabble-rouser, giving a speech on the street one day. My dad had nightmares about McWilliams for the rest of his life. Once a German American Bund, pro-Nazi parade passed Flip's apartment. His brother, Frank, and his friends went up to the roof and threw rotten fruit on the marchers.

It is impossible to know what is true and what is concocted. It seems to me very unlikely that my grandfather knocked anyone halfway across a street, let alone an anti-Semite, let alone an anti-Semite in a neighborhood teeming with anti-Semites. From what I remember of Louis, he was more likely to have grumbled but been too nervous about driving away potential customers to get into a fight.

It's clear to me Flip means, today, to say good-bye to a part of his history, so I don't challenge him on any of it. It's his story.

On Sundays, he says, Louis took him on the elevated train down to Delancey Street where they would stock up on items for the store. It was on these trips to the Lower East Side, at the tail end of the Depression, that my father first became aware that there were places where almost everyone was Jewish. Before heading home to Yorkville, Louis and Flip would load up on fresh pickles and smoked fish and challah and rugelach. And in a brown paper bag, they carried fresh-from-the-oven bialys.

When we hit Grand we turn east, again, and head into the heart of the Lower East Side. I'm surprised how much Asian presence there is in the neighborhood, even as we walk past Allen Street, the traditional eastern edge of Chinatown. Banks and fish markets and travel agencies and groceries, all with Chinese or Vietnamese signage, line the blocks. Only intermittently are there indications—a Judaica store, an advertisement for the Lubavitchers—that this was once an entirely Jewish neighborhood.

A few blocks ahead, on the right, at 367 Grand, is Kossar's Bialystoker Kuchen Bakery. Kossar's is essentially all that is left of a thriving bialy market in New York. Inside the store the walls are bare. A few fluorescents light the place. A woman, not obviously Jewish, perhaps Filipina, serves bialys to customers who form a line out the door. My father is speechless while we wait, almost reverent. When we reach the counter I ask for my bialy with cream cheese.

The counter woman looks at me and says, patiently, "We just have the bialys."

"Sorry," I say. "I knew that."

Flip warned me that the place was a bakery, not a deli. I feel as if I've farted noisily in a library. As I back away from the counter the regulars in line stare at me with looks of both pity and disgust.

Flip wants to see the bakery. He is the sort of person who does not hesitate to walk into a restaurant's kitchen or behind the counter at a department store.

I follow him around back and we find a baker eating his lunch. The baker has the same build as Hans—thick forearms, solid frame, and soft, slightly pudgy cheeks. The bialy baker listens, expressionless, while Flip tells him about our class, his lifelong love of bialys, the deprivation he has suffered during his long Southern exile. Then he shows us a couple of industrial spiral mixers, three seven- or eight-foot-wide bread ovens, stacks of flour bags, drying carts lined with wooden racks. He says the bialys are baked seven minutes after two rises.

We walk outside and stand in front of the store eating. Cream cheese would be nice, but I can see how eating it dry is a purer bialy experience.

We hear someone with an English accent say to her friends, "It's just like a bagel, but without the hole."

Flip steps over and corrects her, though he's gentle about it and doesn't make me want to hide. With his mouth full, he shakes his head a few times and says, "Not a bagel, darling. Totally different animal. Baked, not boiled. You see the onions in the middle?"

A few seconds later Flip is part of the gang, telling them how he used to come for bialys sixty years ago, asking about their travels around the country. I stand by, silently, savoring my first Kossar's bialy, and wondering how a person so close to death can be so cheerful.

When he is through schmoozing we walk across the street and stand for several minutes in front of a block-long, pale gray brick building. Seward Park High School. Flip looks up at the building, but says nothing. It looks to me very much like a prison. The windows are gated. A tall fence encloses the roof.

When he was a teenager he took the train to school here each morning. In the forties it was filled with neighborhood kids and Jewish students from around the city.

Flip starts to cry. I hug him as hard as I can. His chest heaves against mine.

When he recovers he says, "Sorry."

"Why are you sorry? This must be excruciating."

"It just makes me think how long it's been. It's been a very long time."


I've mentioned that my father's visits tend to be short. And I've concluded that this saves us from having to delve too deeply. We stay on safe ground. Flip also comes armed with another tool to keep me at bay. Specifically, he always arrives with a consumer agenda, thus filling any possible downtime in which meaningful communication might occur with slightly frenzied shopping.

Ten minutes after arriving he will, predictably, stop in his tracks and say something like, "Whatever we do, I gotta find a battery for my electric razor."

This trip it's a Microplane. A Microplane is a fancy grater. Originally carpenters used them to shave wood. Now, in all shapes and sizes, Microplanes are used in the kitchen on cheese and potatoes and to zest lemons and so forth. Some

Microplanes are made for removing dead skin from feet. I have two, although I've never tried them on my feet.

Flip has mentioned his wish to buy a Microplane many, many times in the last few days. But we've been occupied with baking and family visits.

Now he stops outside a hardware store on Hester Street and says, "I'll just see if they have a Microplane," and I gather that the time has come. The search is on.

Microplanes are widely available on the Internet and in stores of all kinds, in all areas of the United States, *except* the places my father has chosen to look; that is, in small, Asian-owned hardware stores on the Lower East Side of Manhattan.

At the first stop Flip walks up to the register and says, "I'm looking for a Microplane." On its face the statement is a reasonable one. The tool originally was used on wood, rather than on carrots and Parmesan, so it's not impossible that you could find one in a shop that carries saws and pliers. The problem here is that the old Chinese woman behind the counter cannot speak English or has no idea what he is talking about or both.

He does not give up easily. "It looks like a wood file but the blades are etched in with chemicals." He turns to me. "That keeps it sharp, virtually forever."

The woman frowns and shakes her head apprehensively. It's not clear whether this means they don't carry Microplanes or that she thinks we have some other, perhaps nefarious, agenda. She definitely wants us to leave. She keeps pointing at the front door.

We try again, on Delancey, with similar results.

The third store, on Grand, looks much like the first and second. It's jammed with as much merchandise as Home Depot in a fiftieth of the space. Bags of concrete are stacked twenty high. Everyone in the store is Chinese.

Flip says he's looking for a Microplane. Then he describes it. Then he makes the motion of a wood plane, pushing his right hand up and down an imaginary piece of lumber. A middle-aged man with a cigarette hanging out of his mouth wearing a soiled white T-shirt and a painter's cap fit backward on his head smiles and seems to understand. We follow him into the recesses of the shop. He reaches into a box and pulls out a length of plastic hose.

Flip, agitated, says, "No, no, no" and then launches into his presentation again. The Chinese man smiles and nods. He drags on his cigarette and emphatically blows the smoke out of the corner of his mouth.

We're supposed to go out to New Jersey in a couple of hours to visit with my brother and his family. I'd really like to get in a nap beforehand.

I say, "Maybe we should check out a kitchen store?"

Flip pauses. He looks at me, blank-faced, like he's just woken up, like he has no idea what he's doing in a Chinese hardware store, describing Microplanes to a man in a soiled white T-shirt. Then he exhales forcefully and bends forward, bracing his palms on his thighs. Then he lists to one side and I grab him to prevent his collapse. The Chinese man kicks a box over. Flip sits on it. He says, "Wow" several times in a row.

Because my father says *wow* a lot, and in a particular way, I should explain it. It's not like, "Wow, isn't that amazing." He says, "Wow," but he really means "Whew." He says it in a slightly surprised way, as in "Wow, am I tired," or "Wow, who knew eating all twelve donuts would make me so sick." Flip's *wows* are breathy, usually accompanied by a slow shaking of the head, and are often repeated several times in rapid succession, like, "Wowowowowowow."

"I don't know what happened," he says.

"It's hot, it's smoky, and we've been walking around all morning," I say.

"All of a sudden I got tired."

I leave Flip in the care of soiled shirt man and run outside. I pace the block, increasingly frantic, trying to attract a cab. After several minutes one pulls over. I ask him to honk his horn. Soiled shirt man walks my father from the store, arm in arm. They are the same height. They shake hands.

Flip says, "Mic-ro-plane."

The Chinese guy nods several times, exhales a cloud of cigarette smoke, smiles widely, and repeats it, with a thick accent.

And Flip says, "Close enough," gives the guy a final shake, and crawls into the cab.

# chapter twelve

# Sunday Dinner

WHERE I LIVE there is no snow, no humidity, and no need to take into account the windchill factor because there is no chill and rarely any wind. But I have made sacrifices to avoid parkas and ice scrapers. I have given up snowball fights. And I have given up spareribs.

When I'm in New York I try to make up for these deprivations, which is why Flip and I are sitting at Sammy's Noodle Shop and Grill on Sixth Avenue and Eleventh Street. Probably there's a more authentic roasted meat experience in town. But Sammy's is good enough for me. We order food for six—cold noodles with sesame sauce, a large order of ribs, dumplings, turnip cakes, moo shu pork, orange flavored beef, and a plate of bok choy that looks as if it has been beaten senseless by two sticks of butter.

Over Flip's protest that he'll fall asleep, I order two beers. When they arrive I pour some for him and some for me.

"We're toasting," I say.

"What are we toasting?"

"We're toasting the fact that you're not dead."

"Fair enough." We click glasses and drink.

The restaurant is loud so we sit around the corner from each other at a four top. That way there's plenty of space for the food and I can lean in close to his ear to talk.

When the noodles arrive I toss them in the thick dressing. I serve Flip. He takes a bite so large that I think for a moment some of the noodles might go up his nose. He gets it all into his mouth and then, a moment later, a surprised look flashes on his face. His cheeks are puffed out with noodles. He grabs his throat, shoots out of his chair, and runs into the restroom. On the way he comes very close to taking out a waiter carrying a large tray filled with steaming bowls of soup.

I've been through this sort of thing many times before, so I'm fairly sure he's not having a heart attack. I don't rush after him because when, in similar circumstances, I've rushed after him, he's become irritated with me. As he has explained in the past, all he has to do is throw up. Then he'll be fine. There's nothing anyone can do. It's called reflux and has nothing to do with his cancer.

Still, I'm worried and relieved when he returns, takes a few sips of water, and digs into the beef. The only absolutely sure sign that my father is not all right is when, in the presence of food, he does not eat.

When Flip left my mother in 1970, he moved to a small apartment in the Bronx, near his job at Lehman College. He got a water bed and a white VW Microbus.

In a short time, he started seeing a woman named Heather, who lived in the West Village, just a few blocks from Sammy's. Before he left for South Carolina, once each week, on Sundays, he took all four children to Heather's neighborhood. We had lunch at the Lion's Head, a West Village pub that attracted staffers from the city's newspapers. We went to a penny candy store where we filled small paper bags with fireballs and black Twizzlers and candy necklaces. We sat in Washington Square Park and watched performers like the famous tightrope walker Philippe Petit polish their routines. Often we walked into Chinatown—to the Four, Five, Six Restaurant—for dinner.

The beer goes to my head and I start remembering out loud. Flip is as silent as he can be while stuffing his face with moo shu and noodles and gnawing at the soft ends of pink pork ribs. He does not correct me or add anything. He nods and smiles when I remember Heather's three cats, and the blue and green and red milk crates at his Bronx apartment that substituted for furniture, and the VW. When we took road trips, Flip refused to pull over. He insisted we pee into a dark green plastic trash bag.

When I pause he wipes his hands and mouth, takes a long drink of water, and then recalls the day he took Cullen and Wendy and me to the Bronx Botanical Gardens.

"It was the winter," I say.

"Right. We went into a greenhouse to get warm. Then your sister had to go to the bathroom."

"You said, 'Stop climbing near that water.'"

"You were such a troublemaker."

I was pretending to be a balance-beam walker on the edge of a pond inside a muggy greenhouse crowded with ferns and palms. I slipped and landed in the water. When he returned he roared at me.

It's comforting when he tells a story about an event I remember, however slightly I remember it. Then I know at least some part of what he says is not made up. I was the one soaked with pond scum.

"I don't know what was wrong with me. I just lost my mind," he says. "It was always about something small."

"Why do you think that was?"

"I don't know," he says, dipping a turnip cake in hoisin sauce and cramming it into his mouth.

It's one of those moments. We'll change subjects, talk about the food, about the class. Or we won't.

"Well, give it a shot," I say. "A lot was going on for you, right?"

"One thing I do remember is that I felt very guilty about leaving. I really had no idea what to do with it. And I was so angry at your mother. Maybe it came out with you kids."

I let that sink in for a moment. It seemed a lot like introspection, self-awareness, even.

"Why were you so angry with her?"

"That's too complicated."

Uh-oh.

"I remember you being mad a lot," I say. "One time Wendy and I were fighting over who would get to sit in the front of the van. You came around the front and started shouting like a freaking lunatic." I stand up to demonstrate, whispering the yell so I don't attract too much attention. "*What difference does it make?* You said it over and over again. Like you were possessed." I sit.

He laughs and says, "I don't remember that."

"The weird thing is that as angry as you were, I think you really wanted to know. You seemed always to be confused about what we were doing, like we had appeared in your life out of nowhere and you didn't exactly know what to make of us."

Once again he's like a cagey fish. I had him hooked, momentarily, but he slipped away. Now, as usual, he doesn't remember.


In our house in New Rochelle my mother kept her jewelry in a brown, faux leather case the size of two stacked shoeboxes. The case sat on her dresser. When I was fourteen, I walked into her room and removed the top of the case to reveal a clump of bracelets and earrings and, stuck into slits in the compartment's burgundy felt lining, her rings. In the upper left hand corner were two tarnished gold wedding bands.

I took them and tried to sell them so I could go to a Kansas concert at Madison Square Garden. I found a pawnshop in Times Square, thinking I was unlikely to be recognized so far from home. I was so nervous I could hardly speak when the fat, sweaty man with a bald head and a ponytail said, "What can I do you for?"

I removed the rings from a paper towel and dumped them onto his counter. He asked me where I got them. I told them they were my parents', but they had died. He told me to get out of the store.

I was furious at the fat guy, relieved to be out of the pawnshop, and slightly out of my mind. I sat on the curb and fondled the rings in my palm for a few moments and held them over a sewer grate. Then I dropped them.

For years afterward my mother asked me if I knew what happened to her wedding rings. After I moved to California, I confessed. She said she always suspected as much. I said I was sorry. And I was.

But when I was fourteen I felt entirely justified trying to sell my parents' wedding bands and then throwing them away when I couldn't. I believed my parents had forfeited the right to the rings by refusing to tell me the truth about what had happened between them.

In Cookie's version of the breakup, my father abandoned her and us. He was frustrated because he wanted to write and felt hampered by the responsibilities of family life: the boisterous children, the house in the suburbs, the bills and lawn mowing. So, one day, he packed up his things and left my mother alone with four kids, six months to ten years old. She said his leaving took her by complete surprise. They had their problems, but she never imagined he would leave. She said the day Flip walked out, her life was over. He ruined her.

Cookie returned to the story of my father's desertion relentlessly over the years. She blamed Flip for her misery and wanted us to blame him, too. She wallowed in it when she was depressed. She used it to make the point—a point that turned into a mantra—that men are malevolent and not to be trusted. Cookie's account of my father's abandonment and subsequent neglect—Flip left the state and stopped taking us on weekends, Flip wouldn't pay enough child support—was the central narrative of my childhood.

My dad always said she *threw* him out. Her story about desertion was nonsense. She demanded that he leave and he left. But unlike Cookie, he only gave his version of the breakup when I asked him about it. He never explained why she told him to leave, or why he agreed to leave, or why, once he left, he didn't return. His claim that she dumped him made no sense in light of what my mother said over and over and over when I was a kid—that his leaving destroyed her life.

When I told my mother how Flip had explained the divorce, she said he was lying. Which, I thought, could be true. I knew, even as a kid, that my father was not the world's most reliable narrator. When I told Flip that Cookie blamed *him,* said he had abandoned us, he told me my mother was crazy. And I knew this was true, also.

After Flip left I was effectively an orphan. My father lived several states away. My mother regularly threatened to die, on purpose. I believed, as Cookie said, that the divorce wrecked our family. And yet, the stories of why my parents split seemed totally irreconcilable.

I was fourteen. I believed they were both lying to me. And I hated them for it. So it wasn't really a stretch to chuck their wedding rings down a sewer.

# chapter thirteen

# Sunday Dessert

AFTER DINNER we cross the street to a French café and drink tea. I tell Flip the story of the rings. I describe how it felt to have to live with the opposing stories. I ask him to tell me the truth about why he left my mother.

Which is not to say I expect to *get* the truth. I'm not even sure there is a truth to get. I expect him to say "I didn't leave your mother; she threw me out." That is what he's been saying forever. When I ask him, as I've been asking forever, *why* she threw him out, I expect him to tell me he doesn't know why, she was crazy, she was unhappy, she wanted him out of her life.

Maybe it's the beer. Or maybe Flip figures he might not have another chance. But whatever the reason, for the first time in my life Flip talks about the history of his marriage in concrete and essentially believable terms.

He says the marriage was in pretty good shape when they lived in Michigan. Cookie did her medical internship and went to work in an emergency room. She seemed to love her work. He was an assistant professor at Michigan State. The house was always filled with students. The female students looked up to Cookie, who had no interest in becoming a housewife, who had professional ambition. As far as he can remember, she was not depressed.

Flip and Cookie were in the kitchen once when they heard me screaming. They ran out and found me at the bottom of a staircase that emptied into the living room. I did not appear to be injured. But I couldn't explain what had happened because I was hysterical and because I was two.

"So we stood there while you climbed up a few stairs," Flip says. "And then you threw yourself down to the landing again to show us."

"You let me do this?"

"We didn't know what you were up to," Flip says. "We figured you were an idiot."

In 1967 Cookie accepted a position in a psychiatric residency program in New York. Flip did not want to leave Michigan. He liked his job and the community. Both his academic writing and fiction were coming along

"So why did you go if you didn't want to?" I say.

He ponders that for a few moments. "I should have put up more of a fight," he says. "She wanted to be close to her family, to her mother. And she was going to make a lot more money than me. So what could I say?"

It's not a question. He could say nothing. Cookie had the force of a tornado. It was not possible to fight her and survive. Everyone who entered her ring eventually threw in the towel and fled. She fought everyone close to her, won every time, and always ended up alone.

In the years that followed the move to New York, Flip says, Cookie became focused on money. They bought a bigger house than they needed. She looked down on him because she earned more. She put no faith in his writing.

She compared what he was earning to the salaries of her colleagues.

"Put it this way," he says. "I had a lot of self esteem issues, but your mother didn't help."

"How was that?"

"She had no respect for what I did. She made a lot more money, and we lived at a level appropriate to her income, not mine. I couldn't have supported us on my salary. But money was never important to me. I would have lived anywhere. I never cared what I wore."

This *I* could vouch for. My father's idea of a perfect outfit is anything that keeps his pallid legs, hairy chest, and huge belly covered for less than ten dollars.

"But she did?"

"In New Rochelle she started to care. You hang around with wealthy doctors living in fancy houses, and you expect to do better. Who can blame her? You look at your own husband who is never going to do that much better and you start to wonder."

During the same period Flip was doing research for a book about the Federal Theatre Project during the New Deal. Two years into his research and writing another historian released a book on the same topic. He says he was devastated, but Cookie had little empathy for him.

Feeling depressed and trapped, Flip found a therapist.

"I wasn't very aware of my emotions. It wasn't until I talked about it all in analysis that I discovered how much it hurt. Your mother would say things that demeaned me in front of Cullen, in front of my own son. She was constantly tearing me down. That was when I started thinking about leaving her."

I'm stunned. This is the truth. My father is telling the truth. The description of my mother, of her attacking him and humiliating him in front of others, sounds right out of my own childhood.

"But she always said how blown away she was when you left," I say. "That's the part that's confusing. If she was so unhappy with you, what difference did it make that you left?"

"I'm sure she *was* pretty shocked when I finally left. She was angry all the time, constantly telling me to get out of *her* house." I can hear her, shrieking, her hands clenched, *Get out of my house, just get out.* She must have said this to me a thousand times before I finally left for good.

Flip continues: "But for a long time I ignored it. She probably assumed there was nothing she could do that would drive me away. She didn't think enough of me to believe I had it in me to go, to leave the kids. But I got more and more depressed and I decided the only way to save myself was to leave."

Cookie did tell him to get out, just as he'd always said. But *her* story was no less true, because she never imagined he would actually go.

I am not drinking, but I feel drunk. I am thirty-eight years old. My parents split when I was five. So for more than thirty years I've been trying to understand something that now seems completely obvious.

I think back to all the times Cookie ran people out of our lives. At eight my favorite person in the world was my cousin Lisa. Compared to the gloom that hung in the air at my house, going to Lisa's for the day felt like a reprieve. Her mother was an exuberant woman who had been close with Cookie when they were kids. We saw the family quite often. Then, one day, with no warning, we stopped going to Lisa's. When I asked Cookie about it she said we were no longer welcome. And that was that.

Later, Cookie talked to us excitedly about moving to Manhattan. She was sure if we got out of the suburbs her life would improve. An old and close friend of hers, whose children we often saw, was looking for a place in Greenwich Village at the same time. Cookie found a likely apartment and when she went to look at the place she discovered that her friend had already made an offer. She fumed at her friend on the phone, but the friend held firm. So, Cookie dumped her.

For the first time my parents' stories about their breakup make sense. They were not irreconcilable at all. I thought of the husbands and lovers and family and friends Cookie chased away. Not long after she was always shocked and outraged that someone for whom she cared so deeply and for whom she had sacrificed so much could have abandoned her. With Flip, and with all the others, she was unable to see herself as anything but a blameless victim.

A group of young, striking women moves in next to us. They speak French. My father and I sit side by side, facing the women, sipping our tea.

He tips his head close to mine without taking his eyes off the women and says, "I never really learned to admire the French. Where I grew up we had Germans and Irish and Italians and Czechs. They all beat me up. But I've never been attacked by a Frenchman, so I can't say I really respect them."

"That's insane, you know."

He nods and takes another swig.

In 1974 Flip was still living in the Bronx. I was nine and I had become used to having divorced parents. I didn't live with my father, but I still felt he was a part of my life. Then Lehman College rejected Flip's tenure application. He considered quitting academics. He looked for work around New York, in publishing and advertising. But nothing came through. He applied for a job as the chairman of the history department at Clemson University, in a rural area of northeastern South Carolina. And then he left.

"At that point, I really didn't feel I had any choice," he says. "That was the job I got, so I took it."

"This is the part I don't get. Leaving her, fine. I frankly don't know how you stayed as long as you did." They were married for sixteen years. "But leaving us with her, that was like child abuse. You knew she'd been in a mental hospital."

He nods.

"You knew how she treated you. And you knew what that shrink said about her."

Flip often tells this story when he wants to make the point that my mother was really, seriously, clinically bonkers.

Cookie wanted to be a psychoanalyst. As part of the training, she had to undergo analysis herself. When she went for an evaluation from a prominent therapist in New York, the doctor refused to see her as a student; she felt my mother was too sick, that she needed long-term treatment. This drove Cookie into a rage that lasted for days.

"So you knew all of these things, and still you left her to raise *your* children," I say. "This mystifies me."

I cannot quite believe what I'm saying. I half expect him to dive out the plate glass window or toss his tea at me. But he doesn't even hesitate for a moment before he answers me in a manner that, again, sounds suspiciously like the truth, or *a* truth anyway.

"I couldn't stay in New York. I think I would have killed myself. I was in such bad shape, I truly thought you were better off with her than with me." Now he starts to cry, but he doesn't clam up, which is what usually happens. He keeps talking. His chest heaves. "I had no choice, Sonny. Or I didn't think I had any choice. But it was incredibly painful to do. Those are not good memories." He recovers for a moment and then bounces out of his seat. "I gotta take a pill."

When he returns from the bathroom he sits, takes a sip of his tea, and starts to cry again before he says a word. Through his tears and snotty nose he says, "I know how hard you kids had it with your mom. I live with that guilt every day of my life. Every single day, Son. It never goes away. All I can say is I'm sorry. I'm very sorry."

Watching him cry is almost unbearable. But I keep myself from comforting him by imagining my mother's sullen, glowering face. He got to escape that face. I was trapped.

I try not to cry, but my eyes fill with tears. I truly did not think he had this in him. To say out loud what he did. To apologize.

I have no idea what to do. So I say, "I survived, Pop. We all survived."

# chapter fourteen

# Back to Baking

MONDAY MORNING WE RETURN to the baking kitchen. As we walk through the door Hans is sliding baguettes off a peel onto a rack. In the two days away I'd forgotten the overwhelming smell of the room—the flour bins and cooling breads and fresh liquid yeast churning in the levain machine and seared air escaping from an open oven. I may well die of asphyxiation, but it's the right way to go, like being poisoned by poached sour cherries and chocolate mousse after an eight-course meal at the French Laundry in the Napa Valley.

I sit down on a metal stool at the workbench and breathe hard through my nose.

Michelle exits the retarder with a load of baguette dough. The bin must weigh nearly as much as she does. She dumps it onto the bench. It's thirty minutes before class starts. Besides Flip and me and Michelle, only Laurie and Carla are here. But without a word among us we gather around the dough. I help Michelle with the scaling. Once we get the slab cut up I join in the shaping.

My relationship with the baking room, which was once an alien, intimidating place, has done an about-face. After only two full days of baking, now it feels like home. I know how to find the Artisan Select flour and the cloth-lined bannetons. I've mastered the many buttons on the mixers and the stack ovens. I no longer fear the dough and I have no urge to pummel it into submission. The retarder is still a nice, cool place to visit, but I am not driven to live there by fear of baking failure.

Flip stands too close to Laurie and makes remarks that are disturbing to me, even if they are not disturbing to her, like "How was your weekend" and "That's a lovely necklace." I'm troubled because my father doesn't care how her weekend was and has zero interest in jewelry. He's flirting. Laurie is at least fifteen years younger than him. But she seems to like it, which is even more disturbing.

I step in.

"Pop, come with me. I want to show you something."

"Whaaat?" he says, finishing up a baguette.

"Just come."

I pull him by the sleeve of his baker's jacket and point to Lester, our diminutive African American classmate who stands by the oven with a tape measure. He checks the length and width of the oven and notes his findings in a small notebook.

My father has been stalking Lester from day one. During class Flip regularly comes over to report another of his idiosyncrasies. The guy is definitely a bit odd, but my father's giddy fascination is hard to understand.

Lester bakes with the precision of an eye surgeon. He measures everything: the shaped baguettes, the baked baguettes, the ovens, the mixers, the retarder. He razors off the edges of loaves on a filled baguette loader so every baguette is precisely the same length. If Hans says the baguettes should weigh 300 grams, Lester's loaves do not weigh 298 or 304.

And Lester isn't content unless *everyone's* baguettes measure up; if they are off by a quarter gram or so, well, he's compelled to step in.

He's no less exacting when he's shaping. I'm not a bad shaper and still my baguettes are warped and lopsided. It is almost impossible to roll an eight-inch blob of sticky, gelatinous dough into a twenty-four-inch baguette without at least some unevenness in width and exterior patchiness. Unless, of course, you're Lester, whose loaves are smooth and regular and come to equivalent round cones at their ends, like the peaks of ballistic missiles. I have seen him remake the same baguette four times before graduating it to the oven.

"I've never seen anyone so anal," Flip says. "I gotta go talk to him."

I grab him. "Please don't—"

"Relax," he says, and pulls free.

I watch them consult. Flip seems to be sincere in his interest. He returns.

"What's he doing?" I say.

"He's measuring the ovens."

"That I probably could have guessed. Any idea *why*?"

"He's trying to figure out the ideal length of the breads for maximum loading." Flip laughs, taking off his glasses to rub his tired eyes. "The man's a maniac."


Later in the morning Gabriela, from Little Italy, asks me if I want to go outside for a cigarette break. Flip is busy mixing a batch of dough with his team and I doubt he'll miss me. I don't particularly want him to know I'm a closet, opportunist smoker.

I love cigarettes. I don't smoke very often because I know it will wreck my body and because my wife won't come near me. But if they weren't unhealthy and if they didn't make it hard to hike uphill, I would smoke all the time. I particularly love second-hand cigarette smoke. And the smell of a smoker's car. I love smoked-in clothes and kissing a smoker and sniffing the hair on my arms after a long night in a smoky pub.

I realize these opinions are not widely shared. And I know that cigarettes are evil. But for me the smell of smoke, from the tip of a cigarette or exhaled or even soaked into upholstery, is sweetly nostalgic, sad and comforting at the same time.

My father smoked the way Lance Armstrong cycles. He says he started when he was seven. He smoked at the beach and when he had the flu. He smoked when he got up and during breakfast and on his way to work. He smoked in the shower and when he was teaching and when he was cooking. He smoked while swimming and mowing the lawn and shopping for groceries and on the toilet. My father smoked when he brushed his teeth.

I have no childhood memory of Flip in which he is not smoking. My earliest image of him is from the backseat of the family station wagon. He pushed the electric lighter into its dashboard housing and a minute later it popped out, glowing red. He fitted the lighter over the end of his cigarette and sucked. He filled his mouth with smoke and then puffed out his cheeks one time before he drew the smoke into his lungs. I inhaled with him. He did not exhale and neither did I. He waited a couple of very long seconds and then he blew the smoke out in a single breath. And I did, too.

When I was a kid I harangued my dad about his habit. I hid his packs of Salem and Alpine. I coughed loudly when he lit up. I told him I wanted him to live to see me get married and have children. I said I needed him. But none of it worked.

In his mid-fifties, after smoking nearly nine hundred thousand cigarettes, he stopped. He did not *quit*—there were no aborted efforts or hypnosis or drugs or patches. He told no one. It took his colleagues weeks even to notice that there was something different about him. He just didn't smoke anymore.

Gabriela leans against a ledge of the FCI building on Crosby Street. She talks about growing up in Little Italy, about her romantic troubles, about how hard it is to make a living in New York. As she speaks she holds a cigarette between her thumb and her index finger and gesticulates with it, using the glowing tip as a pointer.

She asks about Flip, how he's holding up. The question strikes me as odd, as if maybe she knows something about his health. I ask her what she thinks of him. Her opinion is the same as Abby's—he's nice, funny, smart. We seem to her to be the best of friends.

The combination of the cigarette—the nicotine gone to my head—and yet another person telling me what a great guy my father is and how close we appear puts me over the edge. In the next ten minutes I unload the abridged history of Flip and me. I tell her he is dying.

Then I think back to what my dad said last night. I got what I wanted, no? I should be thrilled. He finally described what happened to his marriage, in a way that sounds plausible. He explained why he left New York. He said he was sorry.

But I'm the opposite of thrilled. I'm bitter. My urge to punch him out is mounting.

It occurs to me my father has a little list somewhere. The list says

*Things to Do Before I Die:*

1. *Throw out porn videotapes*
2. *Buy additional pairs of underwear so people will think I changed my boxers more than once each year.*
3. *Ditto for sheets.*
4. *Apologize to kids for leaving them with Cookie and moving away.*
5. *Learn to play tin whistle.*

After last night it seems clear he not only invited me to New York to bake bread and eat bialys and talk about his childhood. He also wanted to apologize for leaving and, in his much less than direct way, to ask me to forgive him.

And the realization that my father has dragged me across the country to ask my forgiveness for something I continue to believe is totally unforgivable, enrages me. How dare he ply me with spareribs and walnut cake and mint tea, shed a few tears, and expect absolution for abandoning me, for leaving me alone to be raised by a crazy woman.

He said, last night, that he knows how hard we had it with Cookie.

Actually, he doesn't know shit.

How can he know how she made us responsible for her choice to live and blamed us when she felt no reason to go on. How she unloaded her adult miseries onto us, her endless romantic and professional and financial crises. Where was he the morning I missed the bus because I had to stop her from running out of the house in her bathrobe, drunk and stoned on painkillers? Where was he the day I tried to break down her bathroom door while she bawled that all she wanted was to die?

I smoke another one of Gabriela's cigarettes. I tell her she shouldn't be surprised if she reads in the paper that I've thrown him out our hotel window. She says I shouldn't do that. She thinks he's cute.

Back in the baking room, I stand at an unoccupied corner of a bench working over some bordelaise dough like I'm the young Cassius Clay and it's a heavy bag. Joe slides in next to me at the bench with two unshaped chunks of dough. I grunt a greeting. He watches me savage my dough.

"No so har, my fren," Joe says, smiling. "He no so bad. You no hat him."

I watch Joe for a few moments. He works his two portions of bordelaise simultaneously, one with each hand.

"That's impossible. How do you do that?"

"Practiz, my fren. Lot o practiz."

He finishes preparing the bordelaise and sets them down on their seams. The bread is perfectly shaped, round, smooth. He watches as I try to follow his lead. Mine is lopsided and half-inch bubbles poke out from the sides. If Joe were not standing right next to me, I would certainly find a knife and stab the loaf until it was unrecognizable.

"You do good," Joe says.

It actually makes me feel better, to have Joe approve my pitiable work.

"Thanks," I say. "You do good, too."

At lunch, I sit next to Flip, watching him eat. I look at his sagging jowls and the creases across his forehead a third of an inch deep. I run my finger across my skull and find similar grooves. I strain to remember precisely what it felt like to be me around the time he left. I want to make a movie of it in my head and project my disbelief and heartache for him on the wall of the baking room. I want to show him how leaving me with Cookie was like running me over with a car.

He and my mother argued constantly in the months before he moved out. Cullen and I lived in the room next to theirs and he kept me up talking late into the night, muffling their angry voices. He was four years older and must have had a clearer sense of what was happening. I remember him trying to explain, telling me that sometimes married people decide to separate because they don't get along. He thought Flip would probably leave. I believed him because he was my older brother. But I don't think I really knew what he meant, or why Flip might move out. Parents, even fighting parents, were one thing. Half a tree did not decide one day to move across a park.

The July before he left I sat on our back patio while Flip poured lighter fluid on a lit barbecue. The flames leapt out of the grill and a wind swept them into the side of our house, blackening the paint. I held my breath. My mother emerged from the house and yelled, "What the hell are you doing?"

while Flip scrambled for the hose and sprayed down the siding. She called him a fool, an idiot. I must have exhaled at some point, but I don't remember that.

One night Flip and Cookie had a loud argument and he tried to kick her and instead hit a door and injured his toe. He hobbled around for several days. I looked for damage to the door, but I couldn't find any. The incident made Cookie laugh. She told him he should develop better aim.

Two months after Flip moved out Cookie invited him back to celebrate his birthday. She bought him an expensive stereo system. He pretended to be pleased. Later, after we went to bed, we heard him tell her he couldn't accept the present, that he didn't want anything from her. She cried and howled, begging him to come back. He said he wasn't coming back. I wanted to go out to the living room to cry with her. I thought maybe I could persuade him to come home. But I didn't move from beneath my blanket, the one covered with Peanuts characters.

"You said last night that one of the reasons you left New York was because the other jobs in the area didn't pay enough," I say.

"That's right."

"You said that was an issue because you had obligations to the family."

I suppose I sound like a cross-examining lawyer going in for the kill. I suppose that's why he stops eating and turns to face me.

"Right." His throat catches and he repeats it. He runs his right index finger, back and forth across his mustache.

"So why did my mother have to spend years suing you to get you to pay what you owed in child support?"

I've never actually seen the separation agreement, but I have a pretty good sense of what happened. Flip basically gave Cookie everything—the house, whatever money they had, us. Because she was making more money he was off the hook for alimony. But he signed on for monthly six-hundred-dollar child support payments. Also, he agreed to up that figure as his salary increased.

When he moved to South Carolina his income went up steadily, but the child support payments stayed the same. The arrears added up, so after a time Cookie sued Flip in New York. And just as Cookie involved us in her romantic problems and money worries, she talked to us in great detail about the suit. She painted Flip as a contemptible tightwad who didn't have the decency, after abandoning his family, to pay his fair share to raise his children. She said he was stealing from *us*.

When I talked to Flip about it as a kid he said Cookie was out of her mind. She was trying to get blood from a stone. He gave us what he had. He drove an old car and lived in a rented house and had nothing saved.

The litigation dragged on for years and eventually Cookie won. She waved the papers in our faces and said, "You see, you see what he did to you." Flip owed tens of thousands of dollars. The problem was that under South Carolina law she was not entitled to garnish his wages to recover on the judgment. And, just as he said, he had no other assets. So she got nothing and we got nothing and eventually the whole thing just went away.

"I was paying child support," he says. "She tried to get more money from me, but there was no money to get."

"Were you supposed to pay more?"

"The agreement was six hundred per month. That's what I could afford. She felt I should pay more, so she sued."

"I thought the agreement was that if your salary went up so did the support."

"My lawyer in Clemson told me not to fight it. The suit was in New York and there was no way I could afford to hire a lawyer there."

"But if you could have hired a lawyer, you're saying you would have won?"

"My attorney said I wouldn't win. She had a hotshot lawyer. Who was I going to have?"

"Was she right?"

"Was she right about *what*?" His voice is raised. I've crossed some line, but I don't care.

"Was she right that under the agreement you owed her more money?"

"She was right because I couldn't fight it."

"But let's say everything else was equal. Would she still have won? Were you or were you not obligated by the agreement you signed to pay more money?"

"I was obligated."

My father has been denying this or avoiding the topic for thirty years. I never expected him to admit it. I have no idea what to say next. Neither does he. He taps his fingers on the bench, staring straight ahead.

And so we just sit there, until Hans says it's time to make croissants.

# chapter fifteen

# Croissants

WE GATHER AROUND the benches while Hans scribbles the recipe for croissant dough on the white board. I read in my FCI manual that in the late seventeenth century Viennese bakers, who were working underground, discovered that the city was under attack by the Turks. They sounded the alarm and the invaders were repelled. As a reward for their service to the city, the bakers were permitted to create a pastry they could sell at a high price. The roll they produced, in a crescent shape, mocked the Turkish flag. Marie Antoinette later introduced the bread to France.

I look up at the board and read the recipe.

I turn to Abby and say, "The Viennese must have been rich in cows and clogged arteries."

A croissant turns out to be nothing other than an efficient means of delivering an enormous quantity of butter to the digestive system.

"You have an issue with butter?" she says, not smiling.

"No, no. Butter is good. Nothing wrong with butter."

"I didn't think so."

We mix three kilos of bread and cake flour with milk, sugar, salt, and fresh yeast. After it's combined we add about 500 grams of butter to the spiral mixer and blend for three minutes. The dough that emerges is sticky and smells like cotton candy. If you baked it, as is, you'd end up with a something like a cookie. But just as a goose must be force-fed to create foie gras, the flaky interior of a croissant is the product of stuffing an already lard-logged dough with a nearly equal weight of butter.

Hans uses a wire that would make an effective garroting tool to slice off inch-thick sheets from a log of butter as thick as a fire hydrant. Each of us gets a portion. While the dough rests, we lodge our butter slabs between sheets of wax paper and pound it out into a pane about a quarter inch thick.

Setting aside the butter for a moment we scale the mixed dough and each end up with a half-kilo portion. Then we flatten our dough with a rolling pin so it's about the same size and thickness as our butter. The dough is already so sticky and oily that you have to flour the pin every few passes. Then we lay the butter on top of the dough. A quarter inch of butter now covers a third of an inch of dough. We fold the dough over a couple of times, and then roll it out again to its initial size and thickness. And so, fine, what you have here is an extremely, insanely, obscenely rich dough. But not that different, at least at this point, than piecrust or butter cookies.

Then Hans explains that each time we roll in a new sheet of butter, and fold the dough, we're creating several of those luscious layers in a croissant. It's the butter-dough-butter-dough repetition, which separates in baking, that makes the pastry seem so light and airy when, in fact, it's closer to fried lard than it is to bread.

Hans passes out new butter slabs and we roll them into thin sheets and again lay them atop our dough and fold and roll it out again, and yet again, fold and roll. And then we add another sheet of butter. And then another. And one more. And in the end our dough has fifty layers and contains as much fat, by weight, as it does flour.

I may have to stop eating croissants. This extravagant, even profligate use of butter seems not only nauseating, but also somehow immoral.

I finish and shelve my dough in the refrigerator, where it will spend the night. Tomorrow I'll flatten portions of the dough into triangle-shaped sheets and roll them into spirals so that when baked they'll take on the Turk-mocking crescent shape.

I turn back toward the benches and see my father and Marcel working side by side to complete their dough. The contrast between the men is stark. With his shoes on Flip is five foot three. Marcel is more than a foot taller. Flip is fat. Marcel looks as if he would not fare so well in a stiff breeze. Flip is wrinkled and fleshy. He speaks too quickly and chews too loudly. Marcel's face is unblemished. He has a slightly shy, irresistible, easy, lanky manner. They have the same laugh, though, which comes from the belly and hits every wall of the baking room. I can hear them above the din.

It's obvious when Flip falls in love, because he stops posing. He doesn't lecture. He listens *better,* if not *well.* He's unusually calm. Flip has fallen for the Frenchman. And Marcel seems to have taken to the old man, too. When we work as a class they always seem to end up next to each other. They gab incessantly. Flip turns to Marcel and says something. Marcel doubles over laughing. I'm slightly jealous. Flip hasn't said a word to me since I grilled him about the lawsuit. I have no idea whether I'm supposed to apologize or he is or what.

Anyway, given the tension between us, it's good to know someone else is watching over him. I see that Flip's croissant dough is a mess. His hands are covered in sticky mush. But rather than sinking into the tantrum he threw when he mangled his lavash dough on the first day, he and Marcel are having the time of their lives, shaking dough-covered hands and signaling to Hans for reinforcements.

As I watch them I have the rare and liberating experience of seeing Flip not as my father, whom I love and who hurt me as a child and who infuriates me as an adult. In this moment he is not the person I look to for affirmation and support and often cannot find it. He is not the person I need so badly and am about to lose. He's just a guy baking and laughing with his classmate and enjoying himself.

Becky was my girlfriend the summer before I left home. She had the body of a fourteen-year-old Romanian gymnast, round brown eyes, thick, serpentine hair. Plus, she wanted me, so she probably could have been the grossly overweight, mustachioed female coach of a fourteen-year-old Romanian gymnast and I would have thanked God for my good fortune.

Her parents were unsympathetic to our proliferating libidos. They insisted the door to her bedroom stay open, wide. Her father would check in at unpredictable intervals. Cookie, to her credit, had a more relaxed attitude. So Becky and I spent a lot of time in my single bed, which, amazingly and perhaps disgustingly, still had the Peanuts blanket.

Cookie kept her expensive hair products in her bathroom. Becky and I both had long hair. So we regularly borrowed my mother's shampoo and were almost always careful to return it.

The first time I slipped up Cookie was in a good mood so things did not go too badly. I was on my bed, alone, with headphones on. I saw her come in, walk into my bathroom, and return with the bottle of shampoo in her hand. She combed her hair away from her face nervously, making the point even before speaking.

"Why is this in your bathroom?" she asked.

"Because I borrowed it and forgot to return it."

"Don't." Her face looked pained, disappointed. "Some things are *mine*. Can you understand that?"

I could understand that.

The next time it came up was the Monday morning after a weekend she'd been away. By that point in the summer, most of my friends were getting laid. The promise of a parentless house for forty-eight hours was enough to attract a crowd. And the crowd used up the shampoo.

I found out Monday morning when Cookie emptied the dregs, several tablespoons of soapy sludge, down the back of my T-shirt while I was making breakfast. She did this with violence, not humor. She screamed. I apologized. I promised to get her a replacement bottle. It would not happen again.

Two weeks later, a morning in late August, it happened again. Cookie must have killed the air-conditioning during the night because my room was positively muggy. Becky told her parents she was staying at a friend's house. At just after eight her head hung over the end of my bed and I was absurdly busy above her. If a video existed I suspect it would show an unnatural combination of jubilation and panic on my face. Such is adolescent sex.

The knock that interrupted us was sharp and insistent and quickly became sharper and more insistent.

"Open this door right now," Cookie shrieked, still knocking.

"All right."

Becky scrambled for her clothes and into my bathroom.

"Just a minute. You woke me up."

I peeked out at Cookie, hiding my naked self behind the door. She must have heard us. But she didn't care, at least not about the fact that my girlfriend had spent the night.

"I want my fucking shampoo." Shrieking. "You're not going to treat me like this anymore."

She barged into the room, forcing me out from behind the door. I crossed my legs, ineffectively trying to hide my privates. I might have worried about Becky or attempted to pacify my mother. Instead, all I could think was that despite these distinctly antierotic events, I more or less hoped my mother would go away so I could finish up.

Cookie's hysterics and bad timing aside, she was right. I had the shampoo. She had more than once asked me not to use it. I should have bowed my head ashamedly and returned the bottle to her. Instead I raised my arm parallel to the floor and took a step toward her, hoping, I guess, to back her out of my room.

I said, "Have you noticed that I'm naked?"

She slapped my arm away, and began a new tirade.

"I don't care. I gave birth to you. I've seen it all before. I won't let you treat me this way. No more. You hear me? No more."

Becky climbed out the window and into the front yard. Later she told me she thought Cookie was going to kill me.

\* \* \*

The shampoo was the beginning of the end. In the weeks that followed, at the start of my senior year in high school, our fights became more and more furious. She threw a butcher knife that just missed me. She threatened to call the police. It infuriated her that I was now bigger than her. Now I could physically restrain her while she howled. She felt herself losing her grip on me, and she couldn't handle it.

In late October she sat me down on her orange felt daybed for one of her talks.

Cookie didn't really talk. She cried and yelled and sometimes begged. She howled and cursed. And, quite often, she lectured. At the time of this particular lecture I was applying for college. Cookie said she'd been thinking a lot about our problems. She concluded that they were entirely my fault. I was not, she noted, a fundamentally bad person. Rather, like my father, I had serious mental problems.

This line of thinking was not new to me. Cookie was a psychiatrist. She could say with authority that someone was crazy, even if she had no particular insight into her own problems or possible ways out of her misery. From the time I was a small child she regularly told me that I was mentally ill. She sent me to therapy for a few years with a fat, bearded man whose name I no longer recall. I remember we played a lot of Noc Hockey.

When she sat me down in the fall of 1981 she made sure to tell me that she was speaking, now, not as my mother, but as a psychiatrist who had spent many years treating children and teenagers. She warned me that if I didn't get help I would probably end up in an institution or dead. She said I'd have a terrible life and would likely end up committing suicide before too long. She said she'd pay for therapy, but that unless

I got help, she'd have to reconsider her longstanding offer to pay for college.

I was by no means a happy or well-adjusted teen. In addition to having been abandoned by my father and reared by a suicidal depressive, I was, by nature, a bit manic and insecure, intensely sensitive, and prone to dark moods. But I was not the wacko Cookie described.

Indeed, knowing my mother, I understood her main point was not that she was worried for my mental health. Her point was that if I wanted her to support me financially, I'd have to accede to her view of me as dangerously off my rocker and at fault for our escalating conflict.

Before that conversation, when she criticized me and blamed me for her unhappiness, at least in part, I believed her. After that talk, I didn't. For the first time I genuinely understood the damage my mother was capable of inflicting. And I decided to get out.

I called Flip and told him I was coming to stay. At that time, I had spent a total of perhaps ten weeks with him—over school vacations and summer breaks—since I was five. We had almost no relationship. But I had to get out of the house and I had nowhere else to go.

I told my principal that unless he let me leave, Cookie was going to kill me, or me her. I promised to take college classes at Clemson in lieu of my last semester. I quit my job as the editor of the high school newspaper. I moved in with a friend for a few weeks. And then, shortly after the New Year, when the Clemson Tigers won the national college football championship, I left New Rochelle and moved in with Flip.

\*   \*   \*

On Tuesday nights my dad team-taught a popular class that everyone at Clemson called "198," after its registration code. Flip, then chairman of the history department, felt the undergraduates were woefully ill informed about current events. He instituted a one-credit evening class in which the only requirement was that the students read *Newsweek* and show up. Each week Flip or a member of the department or a guest lecturer discussed a timely topic, adding historical and political and economic context.

I took 198. It was the only time I ever saw my father in action. I sat in the last row of a large auditorium. I told no one I was the professor's kid. Flip lectured without notes. He paced the front of the room, consumed by the topic, speaking quickly. When there was a disturbance somewhere in the hall he stopped and waited for the offending students to pipe down, and then continued without comment. When he got excited he stuck his short arms out in front of his body, inviting the students to share his enthusiasm.

Before seeing those lectures I had no idea my father was so good at anything. Sometimes I asked questions designed to remind him that even if he'd snowed the other students, I knew that some percentage of his lecture was of dubious accuracy. He suppressed a smile when he saw my hand. But most of the time I sat back in my chair and enjoyed the show. I hardly knew him. It was a novel and thrilling experience for me, to feel proud.

After our third day of baking, my father's pace back to the hotel is unusually quick. He doesn't say much. I assume he's still unhappy that I dragged an admission out of him about Cookie's lawsuit.

When we open the door to our room he says, "You gotta use the bathroom?"

"Why?" I say.

"I assure you, you're not going to want to use it after I'm through. I think I had too many croissants."

He smiles and shakes his head. The tension between us lifts, like the fog off of San Francisco. You know it's coming back soon, but it feels good to see the sun for a change.

"That's very thoughtful of you, Father. Let me just brush my teeth."

Mid-brushing he calls out from our tiny kitchen that he can't wait any longer. From the lethal odors wafting across the hallway, I see he's not exaggerating. I spit and flee.

He closes the door to the bathroom and releases a thunderous fart. *Think,* I say to myself. *Six months from now he'll be gone and you'll remember his odors wistfully.*

chapter sixteen

# Medicine

SEVERAL MONTHS AGO Flip visited me in California. Driving away from the Oakland airport, he clutched a small blue and white cooler in his lap. I asked if he wanted to stop for lunch. He said no. He ordered me to go directly to my house because he had to get the cooler into the fridge. Inside the cooler, he explained, was his medicine. He did not elaborate. His grave tone and my shock at his disinclination to eat led me to believe that whatever was in that cooler was damn important to my father's health. I pressed down on the accelerator.

Since that visit I've seen my father regularly and I've observed that he is never very far from that blue and white cooler. During our week in New York, the cooler has occupied a shelf in our suite's refrigerator. I've been careful not to disturb it. I've placed none of our snacks or drinks on the shelf. If whatever is in the cooler is keeping my father alive, well, I'm not going to risk contaminating it with Diet Coke or carrot sticks.

Flip has two kinds of cancer. He has gone through multiple rounds of radiation and chemotherapy along with other varieties of poking and prodding worthy of the bravest lab rat. Thus, I've never doubted my father's claim about the contents of the cooler. People with serious illnesses take medicine. I suppose some of this medicine is not the type you can just keep above the sink.

But I've noticed, too, that he makes quite a production out of taking the drugs in the cooler. It looks something like a religious ritual. He removes the cooler from the fridge. He pushes a button and the handle collapses over to one side. Then he pulls out a small white plastic spoon. Next he removes a squat thermos that matches the cooler's color scheme. He proceeds with such concentration and precision that the process, which might sound commonplace, is actually riveting. He brooks no conversational disruption. I watch from the lumpy couch across from the kitchen.

Flip holds the thermos down with his left hand and unscrews the top, which he places on the counter. Then he removes a small, clear glass bottle, three quarters of an inch in diameter, with a black top. He tips the bottle over into the spoon and fills it with a clear liquid. He places the spoon in his mouth, and closes his lips around it. I notice for the first time that the glass bottle has no labeling.

Meanwhile, spoon end sticking out from his face, he reverses his steps and returns the medicine to the thermos, the thermos to the cooler, and the cooler to the fridge. The spoon remains in his mouth for a couple of minutes. He goes about his business in the suite—changing pants, putting on his socks and shoes.

"What's the medicine for?" I ask, the spoon still jutting from his head.

He sticks up his finger, an indication that he is not yet prepared to talk.

Finally, he removes the spoon, rinses it in the sink, and places it in a dish rack to dry. But still he does not answer my question. So I try again.

"It's for the cancer."

"You mean for the nausea?" I say.

"No. I told you, it's for the cancer."

"I thought you were on a break from the chemo."

"It's not chemo," he says, exasperated.

"Forgive me for being a complete idiot. But if it's not chemo, than exactly how is it going to help with the cancer?"

"Other things can help with cancer."

"Did you get it from the oncologist?"

"A friend brings it to me from Mexico."

I raise my eyebrows.

"I'd appreciate it if you wouldn't discuss this with anyone."

"Will you at least talk to Jen about it?" My wife, the doctor.

"No. And don't mention it to her. I haven't even discussed it with Wendy." My sister, the doctor. "My friend gets me the stuff as a favor. He could get in trouble so I'd like to keep this between us."

"Is your friend Mexican?"

"I'm not answering any more questions. Just keep quiet about it."

"You really ought to mention it to your doctor."

"Thanks for the advice. Are you ready?"

We meet Cullen at the Second Avenue Deli for dinner. My older brother is forty-two, tall and slender, with close-cropped curly blond hair, an aquiline nose, and a faintly crooked smile. I gorge on two bowls of pickles and lose my appetite before the waitress has a chance to take our order. I settle on a bowl of matzo ball soup.

\*　\*　\*

When I moved in with my dad in the winter of 1982, I think I was suffering from a kind of posttraumatic shock. And so I spent my four months living in Clemson in a gloomy haze. There were the battles with Cookie to recover from. Also Becky, whom I loved profoundly, went off to college and found a new boyfriend. So I was in mourning for my first love.

Leaving New Rochelle solved the Cookie problem. But it also meant leaving my friends. In Clemson, I was alone. I had severe insomnia. I wrote long letters to Becky and then destroyed them. I sat in the backyard of my father's white ranch house, next to the garden that smelled of horse manure, and listened to Simon and Garfunkel's "The Only Living Boy in New York" over and over again on Flip's Sony Walkman. I sat in the back of classes at Clemson, trying to avoid notice.

During those four months I began to understand what my mother meant when she said she was *down*. It was not sadness. I felt blank. I didn't want to be in Clemson and I didn't want to be anywhere else. I did not want to commit suicide; I wanted to not exist. I could not see any possibility of ever feeling another way. I thought of myself as inside an immense, pitch black hole, without any idea what I was doing or was supposed to be doing in the hole. And I lacked the will even to try to find a door or a rope to climb out.

I shared none of this with my father.

I felt as if I had gone to live with an uncle. I needed him, so I behaved well, made him laugh, and didn't get in his way. I kept him company on weeknights, sitting on the couch in his office with his beagle mutt named Ms. Pudge, watching news and sitcoms, eating bologna sandwiches and chocolate ice cream. I mowed his lawn. I tried not to do anything or say anything that could cause friction between us.

I applied only to two colleges: Cornell and Georgetown. I could go to Clemson for free, but after attending the university in lieu of my last semester of high school I knew I'd be miserable at the school. I had long hair. I was Jewish. I thought Ronald Reagan was a disaster. I wasn't about to join a fraternity. I had no athletic skill. I read the *New Yorker* and listened to Elvis Costello and was interested in the sorts of girls who might be interested in me. Students at Clemson dressed in orange and went to football games. The girls didn't seem to notice me at all.

The day I heard from Georgetown my father was at work. I got the thin envelope and, in tears, rode my bike over to his office. I closed his door behind me and showed him the letter. I said I didn't know what I'd do if Cornell rejected me. Actually I knew exactly what I would do, which was to jump off the nearest bridge.

He said he was sorry. He also said there was nothing to be so upset over. I could go to Clemson. I would get a fine education.

I was furious. He didn't care about me, I thought. He just wanted to convince himself that Clemson was as good as the other places I'd applied, that *he* hadn't settled for second rate.

But I didn't say a word.

Eventually I got into Cornell, where I was miserable because of the popularity of fraternities, the focus on athletics, and the shockingly high proportion of girls who didn't notice me.


At the Second Avenue Deli I look around and see lots of people, tourists I think, who do not look like they belong in a Jewish deli. They handle the oversized plastic menus awkwardly. They seem faintly horrified by the thought of celery soda and knishes. I recall the scene in the Woody Allen movie

*Annie Hall* in which Diane Keaton orders her pastrami sandwich on white bread with mayo, lettuce, and tomato.

"I don't understand why you're not supposed to have mayo with pastrami," I say.

"It's not kosher," Flip says with unflinching authority.

"Why is mayonnaise not kosher?" Cullen asks.

As often happens when we discuss a topic upon which we are equally unqualified to opine, the volume quickly rises. The diners around us glance over at our table. They probably think we are the *real* Jews, but they are mistaken.

"Of course it's not kosher," Flip says. "It's dairy. You can't serve dairy and meat at the same time."

It's not what Flip says that makes me want to stuff a whole pickled tomato down his throat and come to his rescue only after a good minute or two of choking. It's the tone. It's as if at the tail end of every sentence there is an implied, *You complete idiot.*

"What about mayonnaise is dairy?" I say. "Dairy is milk. Isn't mayonnaise made from eggs?"

"Egg is considered dairy for the purpose of kosher," Flip says.

This is wrong. Or, actually, I have no idea whether it is right or wrong, but I know he doesn't either. And if I've learned nothing else from my father, I've learned how to play the *often-wrong-but-never-in-doubt game.*

"You know I spent a lot of time in Israel," I say. "And I can assure you that eggs are not dairy and they can be served with meat without any problem."

"Well, all right," he says, perturbed. "I guess you know and I don't."

"I guess so," I say, laughing nervously.

My brother breaks the following minute of awkward

silence with an unrelated story about his real estate dealings. He owns three rental properties in a downtrodden area across the Hudson. He is an enlightened landlord—he fixes up the units and charges reasonable rents. But the neighborhood is rife with drug dealing and lately he has come into conflict with some unsavory characters connected to one of his tenants. He feels quite nervous about the situation. His family depends on the income from the properties, but risk to life and limb from the investment seems to be escalating.

As Cullen and I chat about the situation with the buildings, Flip is quiet. He raises his eyebrows and taps his thumb on the table.

Eventually he looks at Cullen and says, "I don't think you're considering your family at all. If something happens to you, what then?"

"If I really thought something was going to happen to me I'd sell them," Cullen says.

Flip says "Okay," but nothing more. And for the rest of the dinner he is silent.

After we say good-bye to Cullen we begin the walk down Second Avenue.

Flip says, "The hardest part of being a father is the fact that no one listens to you. You think you know how to prevent your children getting hurt, and you try like hell to tell them, but they don't listen."

"I can see how that could be hard. You want to know the hardest part about being a son?"

"Sure."

"It's trying to get your father to see that you have your own way of being in the world, and that more than advice, what you really need is just support."

"I'm the father. It's my job to give my sons advice."

"Actually, no. Your job isn't to tell Cul what to do about his buildings. He's about as smart and sophisticated a human being as either of us knows. Your job is to listen to him and tell him you love him and support him in whatever decision he makes."

The moon is nearly full. It's a heavy, humid night and the streets are jammed. We walk through an area filled with Ukrainian banks and restaurants and clubs. I tell my dad that my law firm is representing the former prime minister of Ukraine, accused of crooked business dealings when the country fell away from the Soviet Union. He seems to be only half listening.

"So what if I see one of my children doing something I think is incredibly stupid, that's dangerous to himself and his family? I'm still not allowed to give advice." The question isn't rhetorical; he genuinely seems to be trying to figure out how to be a father.

"I told you what I think. Make sure that he knows you love him and trust him to make the right decision."

A block later he says, "You kids don't know how hard it is to be in my position."

"I think Cullen has a pretty good idea what it's like to be a father."

"I don't mean being a father. I mean being a father about to die."

Back at the hotel. Flip emerges from his room, shirtless, with a black canvas carrying case filled with pills. He sets the case on the kitchen counter, opens it, lines up the prescription bottles, fills a glass from the tap, and takes his medicines.

He stands with his back to me in his tight, black boxers. The skin below his shoulders is pockmarked and scarred, taut, pale, and hairless.

I walk over to him and look over some of the labels.

"Don't mix them up," he says. "I have a system here."

"So the illicit drugs you take before dinner and these you take after?"

"I'm supposed to take the other one on an empty stomach."

"Which in your case is, like, once a year?"

"You think it's nice to laugh at your sick father?"

"I don't know how you keep all this straight."

"My big problem is that with all this stuff going into me not a whole lot is coming out, if you know what I mean."

"That happens to me every time I travel. It's as if I get on a plane and my digestive system goes into hibernation."

"Before I got sick I was the most regular person in the world. One bowel movement every six days."

"Pop, I hate to be the one to break it to you, but six days is not regular."

"I never had a problem. But now it's something different."

"Did you mention the recent clogging to your doctor?"

"No."

A few minutes later I make my nightly call to Jen. I take the phone in my dad's room. I tell her about his problem and she explains it's because of the pain drugs. Like a cement cork, she says. I put Flip on the phone. She tells him to go out tonight and get a laxative.

When we hang up Flip says, "What would I do without my children?"

"You'd be lost," I say. And he doesn't disagree.

# chapter seventeen

# Jacques

IN FEBRUARY OF 1970, I was five. We lived in New Rochelle. My parents were still together, although Flip would leave six months later. Cookie, who was just over five feet tall and rarely weighed more than a hundred pounds, was hugely pregnant. I had shaggy blond hair and women with baby carriages in supermarkets often complimented my mother on her adorable daughter. It didn't bother me. I was quite attached to my hair. I particularly liked the way it hung over my face, which allowed me to see out while no one could see in. I often crossed my eyes behind my hair when adults talked to me.

The bus from kindergarten dropped me off shortly after noon on the twenty-seventh. My father was home, which was not unusual. He was teaching at Lehman and sometimes he had an early morning class and would be home in the afternoon. He said I had to take a nap after lunch because we would be out late that night.

He hardly had to remind me. Like my parents, I was an ardent folkie. I had a record player in my room. I spent hours lying on my bed listening to Woody Guthrie and Bob Dylan and Joan Baez and Odetta and Tom Paxton, practicing my reading skills on the liner notes. That night Flip and Cullen and I were going to Lincoln Center in New York to see my favorite of all, Pete Seeger.

I had a strong, although ill-defined, sense that my parents and Pete Seeger and our next-door neighbor Milton and lots of other people we knew were on one side of a big fight, and Nixon and his friends and kids less likely than me to have long hair were on the other. I knew our side was against the war in Vietnam and the others were for it.

The lyrics of the songs I played again and again supplied my images of the war. I pictured Vietnam, for instance, as a place filled with murky rivers in which men waded and became stuck in the mud. This image is from the Pete Seeger song "Waist Deep in the Big Muddy."

After dark on February 27, 1970, my dad wrapped me in a warm jacket and a scarf and packed Cullen and me into our Ford Country Squire station wagon. My exhilaration at being out with the men for the evening was tempered by uncertainty about my father's mood, which I knew would be strongly impacted by the traffic, first, and then our ability to get parking in the vicinity of the theater. But the traffic was light, although it was a Friday night. And we found perhaps the most unlikely parking space in the history of Manhattan, right smack in front of Lincoln Center.

People streamed toward the concert from all directions. I was shorter than everyone. Cullen walked ahead a few steps. Flip's cigarette dangled from his lips and the smoke wafted down around me as we walked. The lights inside Lincoln Center dazzled against the black sky. I slowed when we passed the fountain and dipped my hand in the frigid water. I don't think my dad saw me do that. He was focused on keeping Cullen in sight.

Flip bought a box of M&M's for us and we took our seats.
After a time a man came on stage and introduced Pete Seeger.
Everyone in the enormous theater stood up and clapped and
stomped the floor. I stood with them and jumped up and
down, but I couldn't see past the people in front of me. I
thought about asking my dad if I could stand on my seat, but
before I could work up the courage Seeger started playing. I
saw no other children in the audience.

I closed my eyes. Seeger's voice sounded just like it did on
my records. It was soothing and made me tired and for a time
I fell asleep. Then there was an intermission. I had to pee. We
left Cullen at the seats. It took us a while to make it to
the bathroom and to stand on a line which extended out the
door. By the time we got back to the theater the lights
were flickering, reminding the audience that the second half
of the show was about to begin.

Seeger walked onto the stage carrying his guitar before the
house lights dimmed. No one was prepared for his arrival
and a murmur passed through the audience. He walked to
the microphone and said, "If there is an Alan Schaffer in the
audience, I regret to tell you that you'll have to miss the rest
of the show. Apparently your wife is having a baby."

The crowd applauded.

That night, when Pete Seeger said my father's name and all
eyes turned to watch us flee the theater, I felt the sort of
bubbling-over proud only a five-year-old can. I have never
loved my father so much.

The next thing I remember was a week later, Saturday,
March 7. By the late morning our house had filled with

friends and family. Our dining room table was pushed up against a wall and covered with bagels and cream cheeses and a bowl of scrambled eggs and smoked fish and a plate of red onions and thick tomato slices and a large orange plastic bowl filled with cookies. Our guests poured coffee from a stainless steel urn into Styrofoam cups.

Flip said the people had come to our house for a Jewish ceremony to celebrate Guthrie's arrival. I'm confident he did not tell me that the ceremony involved the removal of part of my one-week-old brother's penis. That I would remember.

I didn't have much to do at the party so I left. I walked up to my friend Laura's house, a few blocks away. She was out. But her dad, Aran, was setting up a telescope in their drive-way. He explained that it was a special day. For a few minutes the moon would come between the Earth and the sun to form a total eclipse. I had no idea what he was talking about. Aran was a science dad and I was not a science kid. But it was better than being at my house.

A little while later Laura and her mother returned. We waited. Aran looked at his watch and fiddled with the tele-scope. Then the sky began to change color, from blue to darker blue to gray and then to brown. The bare trees and houses and cars looked unreal, like from a cartoon. Aran in-sisted that we not gaze directly into the sky. We looked into the telescope. We could see the moon slowly covering the sun, blocking out its light. And in a few minutes the sun dis-appeared, although rays crept out from around the moon. It no longer felt like day, but it was not night, either.

I understood that the darkness had something to do with my new brother, with the goings on at my house. In fact, I figured the eclipse meant I was missing the ceremony, and might already be in trouble. I excused myself and ran the three blocks home. The bris was just getting under way, confirming my sense that there was some link between the events in the firmament and in my house on Crestwood Lane. I stood with Cullen and my parents while the rabbi recited prayers in a language I could not understand. Then he did something that made Guthrie scream.

I looked up at my dad, who held my hand. But he didn't look back.

"It wasn't Lincoln Center," Flip says.

We're someplace in the bowels of FCI, looking for the Level 2 kitchen, on assignment to pick up the group lunch and deliver it back to the baking room. This morning, our fourth at FCI, we baked off some brioche dough, prepared the usual baguette and bordelaise batches for a first rise, and scaled a few hundred loaves. Chef Catherine offered to accompany us to get lunch for the class, but Flip said he'd been down to the kitchen before and wouldn't have a problem finding it. This turns out to be false.

The school is a maze of look-alike facilities on three levels. When we ask gruff, sleep-deprived students for guidance, they are of little help.

"Of course it was Lincoln Center," I say. "I remember it very clearly. I put my left hand in the fountain. You were holding my right."

"It was Hunter College," he says. "On the other side of town. I got the tickets from a colleague there."

This is extremely disconcerting. I was only five. Perhaps I'm misremembering.

"I distinctly remember parking right out front, near the circular fountain."

"I have more bad news for you. We never got a chance to see Pete Seeger. Your mom went into labor before the show started."

"Now I know you're lying. We have to ask Cullen."

"Be my guest. Also it wasn't Pete Seeger who made the announcement, though you're right the audience applauded."

I stop in the middle of an empty hallway.

"You're killing me."

He shrugs.

"We didn't hear a song? Not one song?"

He shakes his head.

"And you're absolutely certain Seeger didn't take the stage with his guitar and say Mom was about to give birth?"

"Nope," he says.

"Tell me we had a good parking space, please."

"That's true. Right on Lexington. I'll never forgive your mother for that. I've never been in so much pain driving away from a curb."

Just then we walk up a hallway and look through a window into another of an apparently endless number of kitchens. A small group of students in their black-and-white checked pants and buttoned-up white jackets stand around a stainless steel work area listening attentively as their instructor lectures while he slashes into a side of beef. Standing among the students is an older man in a chef's hat. It is Jacques Pepin.

We stare through the window for a few moments.

"Now what?" I say.

Flip leaves me in the hallway and walks into the class before I can remind him to ask Jacques about Julia Child. I see him draw the attention of the group. I see him smile and shake Pepin's hand and pat him on the shoulder. They talk for a few seconds and then a few more, and I start to think I may have to intervene. Then Flip bows slightly to the class and Pepin and emerges into the hallway.

"So, what happened?" I say.

"What do mean what happened? I shook the man's hand."

"And?"

"And nothing."

"That's it?"

He ignores the question and heads down the hall, as if this time he really knows where he's going.

"Come on. I'm starving."

chapter eighteen

# Forgiving Flip

A T LUNCH AROUND THE BENCHES in the baking room Marcel asks me what kind of law I practice.

It occurs to me, at this moment, between bites of my steak sandwich, that I'm ready to go home. I've baked enough.

My fingers are raw and my belly is swollen with carbohydrates. I know the difference between a poolish and a biga. I can operate an industrial spiral mixer, clean a liquid levain machine, and prime a stack oven with steam. I can recognize a properly mixed batch of baguette dough. After scaling and shaping and scoring hundreds of loaves over the week, I can proudly call myself a baker.

Also, from watching Hans and Catherine, I've gathered a few little tricks that will make life back in my home kitchen much easier. Wash and dry your hands once or twice while kneading—the dough won't stick to clean hands. Keep one hand mostly free while shaping so you can easily add a little flour or water if necessary. Add salt last to the mix—the salt crystals slash the gluten molecules and make for a less airy dough.

I'm pleased to have spent a few days communing with my

father. I think we've learned a thing or two about each other. Flip has met Jacques Pepin. We're done.

My mouth is full, so I cannot take the question. I look at Flip.

"He's a criminal appellate lawyer," my father answers.

Still chewing, I nod.

"What's that?" Carla asks.

Carla has come *way* out of her shell. When we first met she could not look me in the eye. When she introduced herself to the class, nervously fingering a feather that hung from her left ear, she said only that she liked to bake and wanted to learn more about it. She seemed slightly autistic.

Because I was not lucky enough to end up on Abby's team I was left to flirt with Carla. At first she had no idea what to make of me. Now, after I hit her with my wet dish rag for two days, made fun of the Garfield pin she wears on her baking jacket, told her she should sue her barber, and swore I once got food poisoning at the restaurant she owns in Up-state New York, she'll not only look me in the eye, she wants to know about my work.

I swallow too much food and for a moment I'm not certain it's going to stay down. Then I say, "I'm not the guy who gets up in front of the jury and says the defendant didn't do it. I come in to represent the defendant after the jury convicts. My job is to make sure the process was fair."

I have been answering the question about what I do for many years. This response is the one least likely to encourage further discussion. Further discussion is rarely productive and often ends up in a touchy argument of a red states versus blue states variety.

Someone once said that trying to explain what a criminal defense lawyer does is like trying feed a parking meter with oysters. First of all, it's impossible, because parking meters don't take oysters. And second, if you try to feed a parking meter with an oyster, you are certain to make a mess. Which is why I have devised a way of describing what I do that is as uncontroversial as possible. My job is to ensure fairness. Most people can get behind fairness.

Flip apparently feels my answer is inadequate.

"You remember the San Francisco dog mauling trial?" My classmates come to attention at Flip's mention of the case. "The lady was held responsible when her dog killed someone? Dylan was hired to handle the appeal, which he won."

"Wasn't there a *Law & Order* episode about the case?" Carla says.

For a moment it seems possible that this question will deflect the discussion away from me, but it does not.

"I watched that trial on TV," says Laurie, sounding appalled.

Laurie is a languid, dreamy sort of person. She does not rush across the baking room. She works her dough carefully, and effectively, but so unhurriedly that we often find her finishing up when the class has long since moved on to a new project. But at the mention of my case she jumps off her stool and points her finger at my head, as if to say, "J'accuse."

"She got off, didn't she?" Laurie says.

"Well—"

"Was that you on TV?" Laurie says.

"I—"

Flip cuts in. "He was on TV all right. I was in Ireland in a hotel. I couldn't believe my eyes. I walked out of the bathroom and there's my son's face on CNN."

"You represented those people?" Marcus says.

"They were horrible," Dave says.

"How can you live with yourself?" Laurie wonders.

"I thought they should get the death penalty," Lester says.

Which, as I think I was just saying, is why I prefer not to discuss my work with amateur bakers or almost anyone else.

In January of 2002, Marjorie Knoller left her apartment in San Francisco with two large dogs. One of the dogs attacked and killed a neighbor. Knoller and her husband were charged with various offenses and in March of 2002 Knoller was convicted of murder. The trial was the subject of intense press attention, which is why the students at the June 2003 FCI Artisanal Baking class not only know about the case, but have formed strong opinions about the character of the defendant and anyone who would attempt to help her.

I work for one of the leading criminal appellate lawyers in the country. Our firm was hired to handle the case after the verdicts. In June 2002, as a result of our work, a California Superior Court threw out Knoller's murder conviction. Because my boss was on vacation at the time, I appeared with Knoller at the hearing, and so it was my face on television when the judge ruled in our favor. Which is why my father saw me on CNN in Ireland.

Now I really want to go home. I've been defending myself in these sorts of situations for fifteen years, so I'm not terrible at it. But I'm tired. I don't want to make my canned speech about how due process must apply to nice and not nice defendants alike.

Before I can decide how to proceed, Flip intervenes with an abrupt and impatient, "That's exactly what people said about Julius and Ethel Rosenberg. That's what they said about Sacco and Vanzetti."

Moments before, I had the ball and was looking at it dolefully, trying to choose whether to kick it, or throw it, or hide it under my baker's hat. Now Flip has it and he's on the verge of a lecture. I know what he means by the historical references, but I'm not sure anyone else does. Plus, I'm disinclined to get into an argument with these people. So I grab back the ball.

"It's pretty simple, really," I say. "Every person has the right to a fair trial and to be convicted only of the crime he or she committed. It's a bit difficult to explain the details right now, but in this case Knoller was convicted of a crime she didn't commit. So the judge reduced the charge."

"She went to prison, didn't she?" says Gabriela.

"Yes," I say. "For four years."

I have to fend off a few more inquiries, but shortly the topic peters out. Minutes later I see Flip alone by the sinks. He looks agitated.

"You okay?" I say.

"I'm fine. But some of these people are just ignorant. I find it astonishing."

He's really upset. And I'm not sure why.

"Believe me, Pop, I'm used to it. You should see how some judges treat us."

"Well, I'm not used to it. I'll never get used to stupidity."

I'm suddenly very pleased. He's not this upset because some of our classmates don't understand the complexities of the criminal justice system. He's upset because he's proud of me, of what I do. It's stunning. The man really *is* my father.

Later my team is scaling out and shaping a batch of bordelaise dough. I sprinkle the workbench with some flour. Then

I flatten a hunk of dough and work it around the bench to get it under control. Then I work it into a ball.

Dave stands to my right. He glances over a couple of times. When I'm about to set aside the dough for a short rest, he says, "You might want to tighten up those ends a little."

"What's wrong with my ends?" I say.

"Little loose there," he says. "You're gonna wanna tighten those up."

I look across the table at Carla, who is chuckling but won't make eye contact. And at Marcus, who can't hear Dave boss me around because he's wearing earphones attached to a CD player stuffed into the pocket of his baking jacket.

I flatten the dough out again and start over. This time I make sure carefully to seal the seam underneath the ball of dough. When I'm through I show it to Dave.

"Much better," he says.

I do not respond.

An hour later, shortly before the close of business, the teams are busy cleaning up the kitchen. I take a moment to watch as my father and Marcel clean the liquid levain machine. They are having the time of their lives. Marcel's arms are covered in yeasty slush. Flip is bent so far over into the machine's steel drum that with only a slight push and a flick of a switch my father could be turned into a preferment. Marcel draws a happy face on the back of Flip's baking jacket in levain.

Abby stands ready with a mop. She has a two-year-old, so I'm sure she's used to this sort of thing.

Dave walks up to me and thwacks me on the leg with a damp dishcloth.

He says, "You know what I always used to tell my students?"

"What's that?"

"If you got time to lean, you got time to clean."

He smiles. He is not a bad-natured guy, but I've had it.

"You know what, Dave?"

"What it is, what *it is,* my man?" His attempt at—I don't even know what it's an attempt at, but whatever it is, it's pathetic. Knowing my irritation probably has nothing to do with Dave, I let it go.

"Nothing."


After class, back at the hotel. We're watching the news.

"Explain something to me," I say.

"Mmm."

"Why did you stop writing?"

"I didn't. I always wrote. I think many of my memos to my department were works of pure genius."

"I mean fiction. Why didn't you stick with it?"

"I was busy with other things. When I left New York I had to run a department. I didn't have the time."

A few minutes pass.

"I was probably just scared," he says. "I came pretty close to a hit with *One in a Row.* But I couldn't end it. I tried a few other things after that, but they were all pretty bad. I don't know. Maybe I was just too scared to try."

A few minutes later I go to the bathroom to change into my running clothes. I stare at myself. I'm beginning to look like him. My cheeks are heading south. The skin on my neck is loosening. My ears are sprouting little red veins. The only thing I have to comfort me as I approach forty is the knowledge that no matter how long I live, like my father, I'll always have my hair.

I walk back into the living area and stand between Flip and the television.

"I'm going to ask you a question."

"Okay."

"Would you please do your best to answer the question carefully?"

"I'll try."

"You would agree that you promised me again and again over the years that you'd eventually let me see the stuff you wrote."

He does not respond.

"That was a question," I say.

"It sounded like a statement."

"Did you or did you not tell me I could see the plays?"

"I may have. I really don't remember. But I may have."

"Okay. And then one day you wake up and decide you're going to throw it all away?"

"That's right."

"It just makes no sense. It's the one thing that really mattered to me."

"I told you what happened, Sonny. When I looked at it again—"

"Which was when?"

"I don't know. A couple of years ago I think."

"How do I even know you wrote any plays? Maybe you're making the whole thing up."

"You'll believe what you want to believe. I can't control that."

"I can't understand how you could want to destroy that piece of you."

"I'm not asking you to understand. There are a lot of things you don't understand."

"Well, then make me understand. Why did you promise me you'd leave them to me? Why did you tell me I could read everything after you're gone? Why don't I get to read the play that kept you away from the night of my birth? Don't you think that might be pretty important to me?"

"I did what I thought was right."

"Well," I say, standing up and opening the hotel room door, "I think it's fucked up."


It's far too hot and clammy for a workout, but I need some time on my own. The sidewalks are crowded with rush hour pedestrians. So I run up Second Avenue, against traffic. The concentration of bus exhaust in the air probably makes this sort of exercise counterproductive. But at least I'm out of the room for a while.

After fifteen minutes I'm soaked and nearly blinded by sweat dripping into my eyes. I stop at a corner and squat down for a moment to tie my shoe. Four large men, in their twenties, with varying quantities of scraggly facial hair, wearing clothing and caps covered in sports insignia, step up on both sides of me. I'm still squatting, so they look particularly large. One has feet twice the size of mine.

One says, "Fucking faggot." He definitely means me.

One leans his knee into my arm and knocks me off balance.

One spits and hits my hand.

I stand up. My head pounds. I turn around and start walking back the way I came. They call me a faggot a few more times.

I don't look back.

This is what it must have been like for Flip. He was small. No one taught him how to fight. He laughs about it now, how he got it from the Germans and the Irish and the Czechs. He calls himself an *equal opportunity target*. But it must have been terrifying.

I walk downtown. On Houston, between Second Avenue and Bowery, I have an epiphany. I stop walking and stand in the middle of a busy sidewalk.

Whether or not he'll admit it or even knows it, Flip asked me to come to New York to tell me something about himself, to show me, in his way, that he loves me, and to acknowledge that his leaving was a rotten thing to do. He wants to say he's sorry. The question is whether I ought to forgive him.

The answer, conveniently supplied by my epiphany, is *no*—absolutely, positively, no. What he did when he left Cookie and then New York is unforgivable. He knew she was a destructive and mentally unstable person who could not manage four children. He left because it was the right thing to do for him, without regard for the impact it had on me. The damage she inflicted over the next twenty years is largely his responsibility. Cookie was mentally ill. I wish she'd been a happier, healthier person, but I can't logically blame her for being sick. Flip has no such excuse.

The very surprising thing about my epiphany, though, is that the answer is also *yes*—unquestionably, definitely, *yes*. Flip does not deserve to be forgiven, but that doesn't mean I shouldn't forgive him anyway. It's up to me. I realize, on Houston between Second Avenue and Bowery, that as angry as I'll always be at my father for leaving me, I don't want him to die with his guilt. Despite his many faults, I love him. Forgiveness, I decide, will be my gift to my father.

"Just let me talk, okay?" I say.

He nods.

"I'm very sad about the plays. I wish you hadn't been embarrassed. I don't care if they were good or bad. They were by my father. I wanted to know that part of you. But what's done is done and there's nothing I can do about it."

He's about to respond, but I hold up my hand and continue.

"I want you to know after all these years of thinking about it, and hearing you talk about it over the past few days, I don't think there's any excuse for you moving to South Carolina, leaving four children to be raised by a lunatic. You knew how screwed up my mom was. And I think, at least now, you know you did something really bad."

He strokes his mustache with his index finger. He has a stern, obstinate look on his face.

"But if I get past being angry about it, I have to admit it all makes sense. I lived with her for as long as you did. If anyone can understand why you had to leave, it's me.

"I can also see how leaving the house in New Rochelle wouldn't have been enough. There's a reason I live in California. I doubt I would have survived if I'd stayed in New York. So, even though I think you knew or certainly could have imagined how bad things would be for us, I understand why you moved away.

"Also, to your credit, since I moved down to Clemson you've tried to be a good father. So I want to say for the record that while I still think it sucks that you left, overall I'm glad you are my father and I forgive you for all your past offenses."

I walk over and hug him.

"Am I supposed to say something now?"

"Not really. *Thank you* might be good."

"Thank you."

"Also, you could applaud." He does.

Which is when I have yet another epiphany. This one is simple. I forgave, which is nice for him. He gets to die in peace. But it doesn't help *me* one bit. I'm still the one who had to contend with Cookie all those years. I feel my jaw tightening. I love him. So I forgave. But I hate him, still. What the hell am I supposed to do with that?

"Explain to me why I feel like crap," I say.

"I really don't know, Sonny. You want to get some dinner?"

"Fine."

chapter nineteen

# The Graduates

FLIP WAKES on our final day of baking with an agenda. When I enter his room to make sure he's up, by the looks of it, he never went to sleep. He has digital camera gear spread out over his bed and he's halfway through a thick manual for his new flash.

He orders me to stand in the doorway while he tests his equipment. I turn around and offer him a view of my rear end, unobstructed by clothing.

"Quit kidding around. This is serious business here."

"I don't get it. You'll take nine thousand pictures, and then what? Have you once in your life ever made a scrapbook or a photo album?"

"Keep still."

"Do you even print out the photographs or do they just fill up your computer until it crashes? This entire thing is an exercise in the creation of e-waste."

"I'm documenting the historical occasion of our last day in baking class. Thirty years from now you'll thank me."

Actually, that makes sense. Thirty years from now I might well like to look at pictures of the retarder and stack ovens and Abby and Hans and remember. Come to think of it, I might well want to look at pictures of Abby next week, but that's a different story.

We eat breakfast for the last time at D&D Deli on Prince Street.

"So how would you rate the experience, overall?" I say.

"Outstanding." He fits half of a bialy into his mouth and keeps talking. "I was skeptical the first day, because I didn't know what to expect. But in the end they really teach you to get comfortable with the dough. I'm ready to go home and bake up a storm."

"All right. And what about hanging out with me for the week? You have to admit, that's been a pain in the ass."

"Not at all. I enjoyed it."

"I ask too many questions."

"You're entitled."

"Haven't you ever wanted to ask me about anything?"

"I don't know. Like what?" he says.

"You got me. I just imagine being a father, sometimes you get curious about what your children think or something."

"Well, I've often wondered what your sex life is like."

Gulp. "You're serious."

"I feel bad I wasn't there to have the sex talk with you."

"So you want to have the sex talk with me at age thirty-eight?"

"Well—"

"No, it's fine. I'm an open book. Mostly I'd say I'm more interested in quantity than quality."

"I want to know if there's anything I can help you with, because I'm very good at it. It took me a long time to learn my craft, but trust me, I'm very good."

Watching my father pleasure a bialy is one thing; sickening, yes, but bearable. This other stuff, well, there are some things I just don't want to think about.

"I can't really think of anything right off the bat." I take out my mobile. "Maybe we should put Jen on the speaker phone?"

"All right, make fun. I'm just trying to help."

"Fine. Tell me what you want to know?"

"You know how to give as well as get?"

"You'd have to ask Jen," I say. "I think so."

"Good. Now I can put a check mark next to one of my children."

"I'm glad I could be of service."

The summer after my freshman year at Cornell I lived in rural Pennsylvania and worked with two college friends at a honeymoon hotel in the Poconos. At the end of July I drove my first car, a bright yellow 1972 Superbug, to New York for Cullen's wedding. The car cost $1200, which was $1200 more than it was worth. The exhaust emptied into the cab. The steering pulled drastically to the left. The engine sounded like the liftoff of the Space Shuttle.

I was the best man. Although Cullen's wife is among the few truly saintly people I have ever known, Cookie was opposed to the marriage. She offered sensible-sounding reasons: Cullen was twenty-three, he and Nancy had lived together only briefly. She thought they were rushing into it. And had my mother been a remotely normal person, these arguments might have meant something. But as with everything else in Cookie's life, her real concern was Cookie. She feared losing her son. She couldn't stand the thought of anyone, least of all one of her children, having even a remote hope of lifelong happiness. So she behaved petulantly for months before the wedding and was sullen and hostile during the event.

At the reception, Flip and Cookie sat at distant tables. It was the first time I'd seen my parents in the same room since Flip walked out of our kitchen in New Rochelle carrying his orange desk chair. It was not so much unnerving as it was un-fathomable. They were like characters from different movies. At some point Flip walked across the dance floor to say hello to his ex. I saw him take her hand. She stood and they danced. Later that day I asked Flip what they talked about. He said they didn't talk much.

When they were through he said, "Thank you for dancing with me."

She replied, "Well, some people learn to make sacrifices for their children."

Cookie and I hardly spoke that weekend. Twice she attempted to engage me on the subject of my brother's decision to get married, and twice I told her I wasn't going to discuss it. I was the best man. My job was to support my brother.

Cookie had always promised that no matter what happened between us, she would pay for college. And while she threatened to pull the plug again and again, she came up with the money to get me through my freshman year.

But shortly after the wedding she called to tell me that she was cutting me off for good. My tuition was due the next week. I had some money saved from the summer, but not nearly enough to return to college. And I was not entitled to loans or other financial aid because my mother made too much money. Cornell was not interested in my family squabbles.

I called Flip, not expecting much. I assumed he would tell me he couldn't afford to pay for Cornell, and that I should come to Clemson. But that's not what happened. He said he'd borrow to pay the tuition.

For the first time since I was five, I felt like I had a father.

On our final day at FCI, we learn a few Italian breads. Hans scribbles recipes for ciabatta and focaccia on the white board. The team structure, which once imposed order on twelve novice bakers, has collapsed. Flip has abandoned his group to climb all over the furniture, angling for the perfect shots of me baking, and the kitchen machinery, and our classmates.

I join Abby and Michelle and we claim the ciabatta dough. I enlist Joe, too, because he's an Italian bread expert. When he agrees to join us I thank him, using my only word of Italian. He has no idea what I'm saying. Turns out he is not from Italy, as I'd assumed. Rather, he's from the Slovak Republic.

Flip stands on top of the bench taking pictures of us consulting. I tell him to go away. He ignores me. The others mug for the camera.

For four days I've kept a nearly constant eye on him, concerned about his health, nervous that he'd offend someone or melt down over some frustration or another. Now, if he wants to traipse around the benches where we're trying to make bread, that's his business. If he wants to set off his flash a hundred times in our eyes, so be it. I'm through worrying.

The trick to ciabatta—flat, free-form Italian bread—is to reserve a bit of water to add late in the mixing process. I've baked ciabatta many times and I've never seen a recipe with this instruction. But it makes sense. You mix and knead the bread, letting the gluten structures form. Then, just before you set the bread into its first rise, you mix in the final bit of water. The water gets trapped within the gluten molecules and, when the bread goes into the oven, it steams up, creating the large, distinctive holes that are perfectly suited to sopping up tomato sauce.

While we're mixing the ciabatta Michelle and Abby tell me they've come up with nicknames for some of our classmates. Dave, my overbearing team member, approached Abby one day and said, "In case you need something, I'm the go-to guy"; the shoe apparently fit.

Abby tells Joe his nickname is The Chef, because he could be teaching the class.

He smiles and says, "No true."

Lester, our classmate who may or may not have obsessive-compulsive disorder, is Puff Pastry, which they say has to do with the delicate way he handled the croissant dough.

Flip is The Professor.

"He's the kind of professor you'd have a crush on," Abby says.

Michelle agrees.

"That's horrifying," I say.

Before I have time to ask about my nickname—Tonto, maybe? I often feel like Flip's sidekick—Hans calls us together to teach us to make handmade pizza dough.

On the first day—the day of the lavash disaster—when we broke to gather ingredients, the room descended into near chaos. It was every baker for him or herself. By the fifth day we're such a finely oiled machine that we cooperate even when we're not working in teams. I say I'll take care of flour. I pull out a bin and start scaling out individual portions. Two others organize portions of water. In a few minutes we're all assembled with our ingredients.

We end up with twelve small, dense balls. Pizza dough is firmer than bread dough. And it rises only once. We park them on a bench and lay a sheet of plastic over them to prevent drying.

While the dough sits we prepare, and snack upon, myriad toppings—pepperoni, caramelized onions, sautéed mushroom, red peppers, olives, garlic soaking in olive oil, a couple of pounds of fresh mozzarella, and pizza sauce created earlier in the day, someplace within the dark recess of FCI, for our benefit. And we open several bottles of wine.

I pour a glass for Flip and deliver it to him while he continues photographing everything in sight. I tell him to give it a rest for a minute so I can propose a toast.

"To baking with my dad," I say.

"I'll drink to that," he says, and he does.

After an hour the toppings and the pizza dough are ready to go, and I'm drunk. Hans tries to teach us how to use our fists to stretch the dough into a disk of even thickness, but to little effect. Within two minutes I've punched my right hand through the dough and have it swinging around my wrist like a Hula-Hoop. The others are not doing appreciably better. Eventually we get the dough flattened out and covered in toppings.

I'm so hungry and so intoxicated that I suggest to Lester, my details-obsessed classmate, that we eat the pies raw. He laughs nervously and walks away.

An hour later, I'm stuffed and ready for graduation.

We sit around the benches sipping champagne and passing around an address list. We promise to keep in touch.

"Well," Hans says, in his languid, amused, faintly accented fashion, "this was a very good class. I had fun. You made some good breads. I think you learned some good techniques how to bake. I want to thank you for coming to the class."

Catherine, breathless as usual, says, "You were a great group. We see a lot of people come through this kitchen and some of them don't even talk to each other. You got along and worked together really well. So you should all be very proud."

We applaud the chefs and they return the compliment.

I've enjoyed myself, but I frankly didn't expect to feel so much emotion at the end of a baking class. I've become attached to the group. We've worked side by side for five intense days of baking. They've been unwitting witnesses to Flip's farewell to New York, to what will be among our last and most memorable times together. More than anything, though, despite my permanently mixed feelings about my father, it occurs to me that I care about these people because they seem to like and care about Flip.

That last bit seems rather strange. The wine may be at fault.

Flip is sitting in front of me. I put my arms around him and lean my chin on his shoulder while Hans calls the names of each of our classmates. One by one they walk to the front of the room to hug Catherine and shake Hans's hand. As at a university commencement, each time Hans passes out a diploma, the group claps.

When Flip gets his certificate, our classmates slide off their stools and stand, applauding twice as noisily and twice as long as before. I haven't said a word to anyone except Gabriela. But they seem to sense that Flip has pulled off something remarkable. He kisses Catherine on the lips, stretching it out at least two beats longer than he's entitled. But hey, he's a dying man.

# Interlogue

There are two sorts of bakers.

On the one hand you have the occasional bread baker. Let's call him Larry. Larry has a wife, a job, a couple of children, and a social life. He's a regular golfer and does a fair bit of handy work around the house. With his busy schedule Larry doesn't have a lot of time to worry about bread. Mostly he makes do with the mass-produced, pale, mushy variety from the grocery store. Saturdays he picks up a fresh baguette from the local bakery for dinner. And each Thanksgiving he lugs his bread machine in from the garage, straps on an apron, and tackles a loaf or two.

On the other hand there is the sort of person who aspires to artisanal baking—call him Dylan. Pictured side by side, it is impossible to miss several striking differences between these two men. For example, Dylan is far better looking. But more to the point, unlike Larry, Dylan bakes regularly and wouldn't dream of buying grocery store bread. And while he understands the appeal of a bread machine—ease of operation, uniform product—he is more inclined to a hands-on process.

More than anything, the difference between Larry's and Dylan's approach to baking is apparent from their attitudes about yeast. Larry, for his part, has never given yeast much thought. When he's ready to bake he walks over to the local market and picks up a packet of freeze-dried yeast. To Larry, the tablespoon of tiny brownish, sour-smelling beads he empties into the bread machine looks like dried mouse poop. So, when a fragrant loaf emerges from the machine a few hours later, he's happy to forget about the hundred million living creatures who sacrificed their lives to make his bread.

By contrast, Dylan, who recently took a weeklong bread-making class at the French Culinary Institute in New York, can think of little other than yeast. He feels as if he has undergone a religious awakening. Real bakers, he learned at FCI, scorn commercial yeast. Real bakers capture wild yeast, cage it, feed it, help it propagate, and train it to do its leavening business.

Dylan always wondered why his loaves smelled and tasted more like *yeast* than like bread, why they weren't chewy, why they lacked the nice big holes found in bakery bread. Now he knows: The shriveled, freeze-dried yeast most home bakers use can't produce superior bread. For that, he will have to find his own yeast, feed it, love it, make it strong. For that, he will have to cultivate a starter.

The idea is simple. Yeast is a type of fungus. It's in the air, in flour, on fruit, almost everywhere. If you mix flour and water in an open container and leave it alone, a few hours later it will start to bubble and give off a pungent odor. Yeast from the environment consumes sugars in the flour and emits gaseous by-products. Left unattended, the yeast will gorge until it is exhausted, and promptly die. The bubbles will disappear and all will be lost.

But if you tend the mixture—discarding a portion and feeding it with fresh water and flour at regular intervals, watching to see that it doesn't get too cold or too hot—it will continue to attract yeast from the environment. After a period of days, a pungent, yeast-dense slurry will develop. Soon enough you'll have a levain, or starter, with which you can make bread. And if you hold back a bit of the starter each time you bake, and again build it up with faithful feedings, you can use the same starter for the rest of your life. You will be forever free of the packets of dried mouse poop. For better and worse, you will definitively be Dylan and not Larry.

It is the tenth of July, 2003. Our cat, Fisch, whose suspiciously timed disappearance nearly kept me from joining my dad in New York, is fine. I have no idea where she disappeared to and she has expressed no remorse over the episode. I've caught up on work and wife and dog time missed during my week in New York. I'm ready to make bread. As a recently converted baking zealot, I know my first task is to construct a strapping starter that will serve me for eternity. Unfortunately, I have no idea how to begin.

At FCI, we drew decades-old starter from the twenty-thousand-dollar liquid levain machine. In New York I quickly grasped the extraordinary muscle of a carefully maintained levain. But I never bothered to find out what to do if you lack both the decades-old starter and the twenty grand.

So, yes, flour and water. But, like, how much flour and how much water? And once you've got your slurry, how often do you have to feed it? And what does it eat?

I try the Web and find lots of useful information, all of it contradictory. Use a plastic container. Under no circumstances use a plastic container. Give your starter a kick with a pinch of commercial yeast. If you cheat by using a pinch of commercial yeast your starter doesn't count, won't be sanctioned by the starter authorities, and will result in bread at which pigeons will turn up their beaks.

I retreat to the neighborhood bookstore and find an authoritative-looking volume by Nancy Silverton, one of the deans of artisanal baking in this country. It seems perfectly pitched, aimed at the serious home baker. It has a detailed section on growing a starter and contains not a single recipe calling for commercial yeast.

Once home I break out my flour, scale, and a large plastic container. I open to a section in the book called "A Lesson in Breadmaking," and read that Silverton's starter takes two weeks. This is deflating, to say the least. Fourteen days seems like a pretty long time to wait to start baking. Suddenly I see Larry's point about the attractions of commercial yeast. But Nancy is quick to reassure: "Don't be put off: You only have to grow a starter once. After that, as long as you feed and maintain it, your starter will be ready to use over and over again, any time you feel like baking, for the rest of your natural life."

All right. Fine.

I turn the page and am thoroughly irritated by Nancy's "Have Ready" list. Among the items I don't "Have Ready" are cheesecloth, a room thermometer, and a pound of pesticide-free grapes. Two hours later I'm back and ready to roll. Carefully complying with Nancy's commands, I wash everything that may come in contact with the starter: hands, containers, thermometer. I lay my pound of organic grapes on a double layer of cheesecloth, tying the corners together to form a pouch. I weigh out two pounds of precisely seventy-eight-degree water, and one pound, three ounces of unbleached white bread flour. I mix them in my one-gallon plastic container. Then I hold the cheesecloth-filled bag of grapes over the gallon container and, at Nancy's behest, "lightly mash" the bag with my hands, "squeezing the juice into the flour mixture."

The grape bag explodes, covering me and my kitchen floor with grape bits. This part is not in the book. I suppose I may have squeezed slightly harder than "lightly," but I'm positive I squeezed no more than necessary to get juice from the grapes, which I believe was the point to begin with. There's no way I'm spending another forty minutes in the car to get a replacement pound of pesticide-free grapes. But the book doesn't say whether the addition of anything other than grape *juice* will ruin the starter, so I spend several minutes picking grape flesh out of the flour-water mix. Finally, using a new, grape-chunks-filled cheesecloth bag, I carry on.

Nancy says "swish the grapes through the mixture a few times, then push them to the bottom." I do that. She says cover the container tightly. Check. And finally, "leave the culture at room temperature, ideally at 70 to 75 degrees." My kitchen is a perfect 72. I stand back and stare proudly at the birth of what promises to be my faithful baking companion for the next forty years.

On the second and third day I'm supposed to see "tiny bubbles in the mixture, and the bag of grapes may have begun to inflate." I wake up the next morning, run to my starter, and see bubbles. But not inflation. This doesn't seem like a big deal, particularly because my exploding grape situation may have queered that part. Also, Nancy says to smell the mixture: "You should notice a fruity or yeasty aroma." To me it just smells nasty, but if I stretch I suppose I can say it smells sort of fruity-nasty.

By the fourth day, according to the book, the mixture will look "brownish purple." "A distinct, unpleasant, alcohol-like smell should be present, and the culture will taste sharp and acidic." I certainly smell what I'm supposed to smell, and see the brownish purple mush she describes. I have my doubts that anyone, including Silverton, ever dared to taste starter at this stage. It looks like decaying flesh. I take her word on taste and follow her instructions to refresh the starter with half a pound of water and four ounces of flour.

On days five through nine the yeast is busy developing. The book says, essentially, do nothing. This instruction I can follow perfectly.

On the tenth day begins the critical period of refreshing and intensifying. My mixture contains plenty of yeast, but it's like an infant—unmistakably alive, smelly as hell, and unable to fend for itself. Only by repeatedly discarding most of the culture and adding fresh flour and water will I end up with an adult starter, able to rise a loaf of bread.

It is not until I read Nancy's care and feeding instructions, and begin the process, that I grasp how fitting the infant metaphor is. The starter requires feeding three times each day, and stirring between feedings, which means I have to tend to the thing every three waking hours. This seems suspiciously like a breast-feeding schedule, and I make a note to check if Nancy Silverton has children.

In the meantime, I comply. At eight a.m. I discard most of the mix and add flour and water. At eleven I stir. At two I add twice as much flour and twice as much water. At four I stir. At seven, again, I double the amount of flour and water. The starter has thus consumed nearly four pounds of flour today. At ten I stir.

Then I go to bed.

There, I excitedly tell Jen that I feel as if my starter marks the beginning of a new phase in my life—a more thoughtful, live-in-the-moment, appreciate-the-everyday phase. Once my starter is done I intend to bake several times each week. I'll give away the bread to the homeless. I'll be more charitable, less frenetic. I feel making bread routinely, using my new starter, will provide some balance to my life.

But going to bed turns out to be a big mistake because my starter, as reliably as any other infant, makes an unholy mess when it eats. I rush downstairs the next morning to begin the feeding process anew, only to find my kitchen counter, floor, and cabinets covered in levain. My Silverton book is also soaked, which seems deserved, somehow.

Jen returns from the morning dog walk. The mess and my frustration amuse her. She says, "Who knew having a balanced life was so disgusting." Then she releases the dogs and they assist with the clean up.

I make adjustments—store my container in an enormous bowl that collects the spillover—and by day fifteen I have a starter. I plunge my hand into it and it crackles. It smells sweet, just like the levain at FCI. I am proud, like a father watching his son walk across a field to accept his Little League trophy.

Maybe this is why people preserve their starters forever, why the levain at FCI has been around for thirty years and will last another several hundred at least. It *is* something like having a child. It's totally reliant on you for its life.

Every day you have to make a choice: Should I feed it or let it die? Caring about and committing to something other than yourself—even if it is just a container of yeasty sludge—seems among the truly consequential things you can do with your life.

It reminds me that my father made a very different choice when it came to his children, which may have something to do with why the idea of the levain at FCI was slightly unnerving for me. It may also have something to do with the fact that I am extremely reluctant to have my own children. Can I commit? Would I do what Flip did?

I turn a few pages forward in the Silverton book and find a recipe for "The Basic Loaf." Nothing too ambitious to start. I clear my workspace and prepare to solo for the first time, to bake my first truly legitimate loaf of bread.

Then the phone rings.

It's my brother Cullen. He's been on the phone with my dad, my stepmother, and other family members. Flip's latest CAT scan shows bone and liver metastases. Jane describes a different person than I left at the airport in New York five weeks ago. He sleeps all the time. He hardly eats. It sounds to me like my father is finally dying.

I call.

"Hi, Sonny." He sounds like a stranger. He sounds indifferent.

"I'm going to come visit," I say.

"When?"

"Now. Tomorrow."

"Please don't do that."

"Why not?"

"I don't need anyone to take care of me," he says.

"I'm coming to take care of me, not you."

"All I do is sleep. What are you going to do?"

"I'll be fine. I'll call you when I get in."

Long exhale, through the nose. "All right. I'm going back to bed."

In the fall of 2000, a few months before I learned that my father had cancer, my friend Josh called me in California. He was in New Rochelle. His mother, Jane, was about to die. He said if I wanted to say good-bye, I should fly out.

I spent a lot of time at Josh's house in my teenage years, and I figured I should go, to say good-bye to Jane, and to support my friend. I had a particular attachment to Josh's family because they took me in for a month, in the middle of my senior year in high school, when my relationship with Cookie finally disintegrated. And they took me in, during my junior year in college, after my mother had me arrested.

That October I spent two days at Jane's house and several hours in her room. She seldom spoke. She was skeletal, took each shallow breath with great difficulty, and seemed minimally aware of what was happening around her. But there was something surprisingly and inexplicably thrilling and magnificent about her progression away from life. It was more than the love of her family and friends. It was more than the drama of a life ending. It was the dying itself that drew me, like a thousand-foot ledge that demands peering over. I left New Rochelle that weekend knowing that if I had the chance, if my father ever became critically ill, I would drop whatever I was doing and fly to South Carolina so I could be with him at the end.

I spend the day making arrangements, covering work projects, canceling appointments. I'm not coming back to Oakland until my dad dies, and I have no idea how long that's going to take—months maybe.

The next morning everything is in order. Jen and dogs wait at the door to say good-bye. At the last minute something occurs to me. I walk to the kitchen, open the gallon plastic container, inhale deeply, and dump my levain into the garbage.

# South Carolina

*Senza il pane tutto diventa orfano*
Without bread, everyone is an orphan

**—Italian proverb**

# chapter twenty

# Arriving

I ENTER THE BELLIGERENTLY AIR-CONDITIONED Green-ville-Spartanburg Airport a few minutes past nine p.m. Except for the deplaning passengers the terminal is empty. It looks like the after-hours lobby of an insurance company—gleaming floors, long rows of windows, bad art. I need to call Flip before I get on the road. I stretch out on a row of black faux leather seats and stare up at a triptych of twenty-foot-high abstract paintings covered with colossal swaths of red and orange. The work is bloody and explosive and seems not only bad but also inappropriate for an airport.

I turn on my mobile. A message on the screen reminds me I'm roaming, which is precisely how I feel. I phone my dad to tell him I'm in, but the answering machine picks up. It says, as it has for as long as I can remember, "You've probably reached the number you dialed."

The air outside the terminal doors smells like a heap of rotting roses. In fact, during the summer the entire north-eastern chunk of South Carolina—the Piedmont, because it sits at the foot of the Blue Ridge Mountains—is like the world's biggest compost pile, moldering and sodden and earthy-sweet.

The drive to Clemson takes about forty-five minutes. Much of it is off the Interstate, on two-lane county roads lined with Wal-Mart stores and Long John Silver's and furniture distributors and real estate outfits and car dealerships. And churches. Every time I return to the south I'm struck by the enormous number of places of worship for Christians, and how weird it is that my Jewish father has lived here for a third of his life. Some are small, stuck into strip malls between "Oriental" restaurants and hot tub outlets. Some spread across intersections and into surrounding neighborhoods and up into the sky with crosses the height and girth of an up-ended 747.

Ten minutes from Flip's house the lights and commerce trail off and the road winds through an impenetrable thicket of pine and kudzu. There are no streetlights and no moon. There are few vehicles. It's even hotter and wetter than in Greenville.

I pull into Flip's driveway and his dog, Ginger, a ninety-pound rust-colored mutt, launches herself against the rental car. My rented Escort is no match for the dog. It rocks back and forth precariously and looks set to roll over when I slam the door into Ginger's midsection, buying myself a few moments, and exit the vehicle. The dog snarls at me but she can't keep her tail from wagging, so I know it's a shallow pose. I bark back and she retreats to her house.

I feel sorry and walk over to her residence—an amiable little structure Flip built. It's filled with cedar chips and a couple of pillows and some old bones. I pet her for a minute, looking at the mostly dark windows on my father's house, and think how strange it is, that this will be the last place he lives.

And he lives alone. He married Jane in the mid-seventies. Her house and work were in Atlanta. His were two hours away, in Clemson. They get together on weekends and holidays and they seem to still like each other after twenty-five years.

I walk up to the front door and stand there for several minutes. I can hear my heart in my ears. I can't quite catch my breath. I feel exactly this way just before I present an argument to the Court of Appeal—nervous and excited, like I'm about to do something I'm not at all qualified for. I knock. There is no answer. I try again. I can hear the television. Nothing. This time I hit the door hard enough to scrape a bit of skin off the knuckle of my ring finger. I hear Flip grumbling inside.

"Okay, all right already. Take it easy."

The door opens.

In the past three years I've thought to myself hundreds, maybe thousands of times, *Flip is dying, he will be gone soon, there is nothing I or anyone can do about it.* I have had this conversation with my wife and my brothers and my stepmom. And I've discussed it all with my father. But this is the first time I really get it. He has never looked old before. Now his shoulders slump so far forward he looks like he's about to topple over. He's lost at least fifty pounds. His unshaven cheeks are sunken. He shuffles his feet along the floor as he moves, toward the living room couch, and caves into it like it's taken his last ounce of energy to answer the door.

More than anything, though, it's what he's wearing. Until tonight, I have never, ever seen my father in a bathrobe. He sleeps naked and dresses first thing in the morning. He has no use for transitional attire. Robes are for people who relax. The day Flip Schaffer started to relax was the day he began to die.

He stares at the television but doesn't really seem to be watching. I can't tell whether he's stoned on painkillers or half asleep or whether the sight of me is just too hard. But during the entire conversation he doesn't look at me once.

"How are you doing?" I say.

"Incredibly tired."

"Go to sleep. I'll still be here in the morning."

"That's what I'm worried about." He still makes no eye contact. "I wanted to make sure you got in okay."

"I'm fine."

"How was the trip?" he says.

"No problems. Can I get you anything?"

He looks past me and then returns to the television.

"Where's your bag?"

"In the car. I'll get it in the morning."

"How long are you staying?"

"I'm here seven minutes and already you're trying to get rid of me?"

"I don't need anyone taking care of me."

"You've made that very clear. Believe me," I say, walking into the kitchen to make tea, "the last thing I want to do is take care of you."

A few minutes later he shuffles off to his room. When I hear him snoring I go out to the car and retrieve my super-sized luggage, roll it as quietly as I can into the guestroom, and hide it in a closet.


I'm on California time so there's no way I'm going to sleep any time soon. After I've cycled twice through the three hundred channels on my father's satellite television, I wander into the kitchen to explore. Flip has amassed hundreds of dollars of baking accessories and ingredients, all of them unused. I decide to prepare an overnight dough for baking in the morning.

I do the bread by hand, on a large cutting board. I put in my earphones and crank up my iPod. The lights are out in the house except for the kitchen and it feels as if I'm the host of a television cooking show, baking bread for a studio audience and millions watching from home. I pretend to mug for the camera, squeezing the ingredients through my fingers like a four-year-old in a mud pile and tipping the board forward to show the nonexistent studio audience what a mess I've made.

I sing along to the music, dance feverishly in place, and then spin to my right. Flip is standing inches from me, naked. He scares the hell out of me and I yelp and catch my earphone wires on the knob of a cabinet below the counter and rip the phones from my ears and the iPod from my waist. When I recover I see that he is at best a quarter awake.

"What's wrong?" I say.

"Huh?"

"What are you doing?"

"Standing here."

"That I can see. Aren't you cold?"

Like all indoor areas in the south in July, Flip's house feels like the inside of a hockey rink.

"What?"

His hands, hanging down at his sides, are trembling. Mine are covered in sticky dough, so I feel his right wrist with my own. It's icy. I walk over to the sink and clean up.

"Don't you think you should go back to bed?" I say.

His eyes track me across the room as I walk back to him, but he does not move.

"You want to help me bake?"

"Huh?"

"Nothing."

"I gotta go to bed," he says.

"Who's stopping you?"

He shuffles off without another word.

# chapter twenty-one

# Pee

WHEN I WAS FOUR, living in New Rochelle, my father crossed the street to talk to our neighbor Mr. Kaufman. He took me along. Mr. Kaufman, like Flip, was short. His wife had curly blond hair. He was an accountant and so, unlike my father, who was a history professor and a writer, Mr. Kaufman was clean-shaven and had neatly trimmed hair. The Kaufman family lived at the top of a steep driveway. I held my dad's hand as we climbed up to the front door. My legs were so short and so fat that it was as if my feet were attached directly to my ass. We made slow progress up to the house.

When we reached the front door Flip let go and shifted his cigarette into the hand that had held mine. He waited a few moments to catch his breath. Then he knocked. Mrs. Kaufman answered. I had to go to the bathroom. Mr. Kaufman appeared. The men stepped away from the house, onto a hedge-lined concrete walkway, and began a conversation. It was a friendly discussion, but it was not just a chat. There was a question that required resolving. It had something to do with a lawn mower. Lawns and their care were a serious matter in our enclave of first-generation Jewish suburbanites. After a few minutes my need to pee had increased substantially. I had been trained to inform an adult when I had to use the bathroom. So, now, I reached up and tapped my father's arm. I don't know whether he felt it or not, but he did not respond. I looked at him for a few seconds while he spoke, gesticulating with his cigarette-holding left hand. Then I tried again. This time he said, "Hold on. We're in the middle of something."

I waited another minute and tried again. And again I was unable to break into the conversation. I suppose I could have just walked into the Kaufmans' house and asked Mrs. Kaufman if I could use the bathroom. I can't say why I didn't do that.

Instead, I peed on Mr. Kaufman's feet. Before Mr. Kaufman noticed and stepped aside, I'd pretty well soaked his loafers. In retrospect I feel rather bad about the episode. I really ought to have aimed for my dad, since he was the one ignoring me. But I distinctly recall feeling that Flip was not the person to blame.


At seven my first morning in Flip's house the dog slams her paws into the guestroom window inches from my head. The room is quite dark. It takes me a minute to remember where I am, and to figure that it's Ginger and not someone jackhammering my dad's foundation.

I walk into the hallway bathroom. The wallpaper is peeling off in foot-long sheets. The toilet and bathtub have not been cleaned in a very long time. The vinyl floor, too, is coming unglued. It's covered in a layer of oily, dusty, hairy grime.

Flip is in the kitchen. He asks if I wouldn't mind feeding the dog. I know asking me pains him, so I don't scream during his half-hour lecture on the subject of *how* to feed Ginger.

When I walk outside the soggy heat enshrouds me. The sky is ashen. I walk across Flip's overgrown lawn to Ginger's house. Although she is twice my age (according to the usual formula for measuring dog years), the heat doesn't seem to bother her. She bounds in and out of the bed of a half-dead pickup in the driveway until she sees where I'm heading and then paces the yard until I deliver her breakfast.

I turn around to survey the house. The windows look as if they have not been cleaned since they were installed. Those by the front door are caked with red clay. Debris chokes the gutters. The roof, covered in dark stains, seems ready to blow off in the next bad storm. A copse of tall grasses and ivy and low-hanging trees appears to be waiting for my father to depart before it swallows the house.

I walk down the driveway and halfway up the block. Flip lives on a cul-de-sac in a small development about a fifteen-minute drive from the Clemson University campus. The homes are from the seventies—boxy, bland, wood-sided. The landscaping is indifferent—flowerboxes with wilting lilies, anemic shrubbery.

When I return Flip meets me at the door. He says he has an appointment with his urologist in Anderson, a twenty-five-minute drive. He says I can come if I want. "Sure," I say, trying not to react. "I'd like that."

The thought that, had I not arrived yesterday, he would have driven himself to this appointment is terrifying. He moves at the pace of a sloth. He cannot walk more than twenty feet without having to sit. His hearing is worse than ever.

I ask if he wants me to make breakfast. He says he'll have a bagel. I suppose it's impossible to get a decent bialy in these parts. I open the refrigerator.

Which is when I remember my dough. Seven hours earlier I'd stowed it in a bowl and covered it with a sheet of plastic wrap. My idea was that the refrigerator would function like the room-size retarder at FCI—the dough would develop slowly, developing a rich taste and firm, chewy structure. This worked perfectly in New York. Not so in South Carolina. Maybe it's the humidity, or some other atmospheric variable of which I'm unaware. The low temperature does not seem to have retarded anything.

The dough has oozed out of the bowl, across an entire shelf, and down into the fruit drawer. I ought to be rushing to clean up the mess before Flip discovers it, but I'm bewildered by the disappearance of the plastic wrap that once covered the bowl. I poke around in the piles of dough until I find it, buried, between a bag of carrots and a carton of eggs.

I toast a grocery store bagel for Flip.

Sitting at the table, he says, "You're not eating?"

"It's five in the morning for me." I pluck half of his bagel off his plate and hold it up for inspection. "Anyway, I don't know how you can eat these things. They don't even qualify as bread, let alone bagels."

"That's all we have down here."

"You should have opened up a bagel store. You would have made a bundle."

"I thought about it."

I lather the bagel with margarine. Flip pushes his chair away from the table. I jump up.

"What do you need?" I say.

"Coffee."

"I'll do it." If he opens the fridge I'm in trouble.

"I can still make coffee."

"Poppala, sit. What good are children if they don't wait on you hand and foot?"

I take out the milk. It's about two-thirds solid.

"The milk's bad," I say.

"What are you talking about? I just bought that."

"It's fine if you want yogurt in your coffee."

"Don't throw it away. I'll save it for Ginger."

"I see you're planning to kill the dog before you go. Very Egyptian of you."

He fakes a smile, takes a few unenthusiastic bites, and is through.

On the way home from his urology appointment Flip reports that his doctors agree it's time to take a break from the treatments. No more chemo for a while. No more radiation.

"We'll see how things look in a month or two and then I'll decide what next."

"That sounds reasonable," I say.

I don't know whether he's reporting the discussions accurately. But, this morning, for the first time in my life, I saw my father leave food on a plate. Nothing any doctor says could better convince me that my father is on his way out.

Thirty-four years after relieving myself on Mr. Kaufman's shoes, I'm standing in my father's wood-paneled dining room watching him pee into an orange plastic cup. Clemson's teams are the Tigers, their color, orange. Flip isn't much of a fan, but the cups come free with gas fill-ups and groceries. The bathroom is just down the hall, perhaps twenty feet away, but I guess the cup works, too.

It's after nine at night. He's by the kitchen sink. His head is bent over, ensuring he doesn't miss. His left arm hangs by his side, as does a velour belt sewn into his robe. The cancer has inundated his bladder, making it harder and harder for him to urinate. On the other hand, he has to go all the time and with great urgency. This must be why he's peeing in a cup. He probably couldn't get to the bathroom in time.

Flip is fond of the story about Mr. Kaufman; he tells it regularly. Another model of father would have been mortified, anxious about his standing in the neighborhood. Instead, at least in the retelling, my dad always seems proud.

I like it, too. The story reminds me that I once loved him without reservation. At four, I could not imagine that my father could be to blame for anything.

Flip finishes. I wonder what he intends to do with the cup. Should I offer to carry it to the bathroom? He steps up to the sink and empties it. He rinses out the cup, but he does not use soap. He does not wash his hands. He does not set the cup apart from the ones used for drinking.

I say nothing.

Flip and I never had the chance to begin a dialogue about these things, about being a man, about male parts and problems, about how our bodies betray us when we get old. I learned about sex and the little I know about sports and cars and power tools without him.

What are you supposed to say to your dying father when you see him peeing in a cup? "You want me to hold that for you?" "Wouldn't you rather use a Gamecocks cup?" The Gamecocks are the team from the University of South Carolina, Clemson's archrival.

He turns, slowly enough that I have time to back into the dining room, sit, and pretend to be reading.

"You okay?" I say, when he enters.

"Mmm," he says and walks down the hall to his room.

I tiptoe to the sink and squeeze a third of a bottle of dishwashing liquid into it. I run scalding water around the basin and down the drain for two minutes. Then I open the window above the sink and flick the cup into the yard.

chapter twenty-two

# Shrimp Tales

O  N MY SECOND DAY Flip gets up around nine. He shuffles into the dining room and sits at a table crowded
with piles of books and papers.

He says, "Wow." Then he fills his cheeks with air and exhales loudly. "I slept ten hours and I'm still exhausted."

"You're sick," I say.

"Wowowowow."

He sits at the table and stares at the wall. I walk over and
rub his shoulders for a moment.

"Can I clear off some of the stuff?" I say. "It might be nice
to be able to actually *eat* in here."

I suggest we move the piles to a table across the room. He
says no. He has to get to work, to deliver the documents to
his secretary before the semester starts. Flip has managed to
work harder in retirement—recently on rewriting the faculty
senate manual—than during his career. But now there's no
chance he'll get to any of it. I doubt he'll ever leave the house
again. He lets me clear the books onto the floor. Sandwiched
between two library books is a manila envelope that contains
a draft of my book.

At the end of 2001 I quit my full-time job as a lawyer to

write. I wrote a couple of novels I couldn't sell. Along the way I interested an agent in my work. Shortly before the baking class she called to tell me she liked my latest, and that she would try to sell it.

"So, did you ever get to this?" I say, holding up the envelope.

"I haven't had the time. It looks pretty interesting."

"You should read it."

"I'll read it."

"Before you die or after?"

"I'll send you a critique."

"I don't want a critique."

"I'm the father so I'll send you a critique. That's my role in life."

The toast is from the baguettes I made yesterday. Without the ancient levain and stack ovens and retarder and the other commercial equipment they don't look anything like the loaves we made in New York. The crust is pale, not golden and shiny. And the crumb is far tighter than in an authentic baguette. But given the tools and ingredients, I haven't done a terrible job. The bread tastes pretty good.

Flip takes a few bites and a few sips of tea and then sits in silence for another five minutes staring at a paneled wall. Then he says "wow" a few times and slowly rises from the table and goes back to bed. I clean up from breakfast. Every fifteen minutes or so I walk into his room and sit on the edge of his bed and put my hand to his mouth to make sure he's still breathing. I do his laundry. I walk Ginger. I mow the lawn.

Late in the day Cullen arrives in a small white rental car. Flip emerges from his room just long enough to say hello.

\* \* \*

A dying person should have an indicator, like a fuel gauge in a car, which says how long he has. It doesn't have to be too accurate. You never *really* know when your car is going to conk out. But when the little white needle crosses the little red "e," at least you know you need to start thinking seriously about finding a gas station.

Or perhaps a dying man could have one of those convenient pop-up tabs that come with Thanksgiving turkeys.

Anyway, my problem is that I have no idea how long I'm going to be here. If I knew Flip was going to die this week, I wouldn't bother trying to turn his house into a place where I can live. As it stands, the house is more the sort of place you might visit, once, and then tell nauseating stories about for the rest of your life.

On the other hand, if he *is* going to hang on, I have an enormous amount of work to do.

The tub, once white, now is the color of a Brillo pad long past its prime. A third of an inch of greasy dust covers nearly every surface in the house. The Venetian blinds in my room sag with grime. I will not embarrass my father by describing what I find in and around the toilet in the guest bathroom.

The refrigerator would fit right in at the Whitney Biennial. If Flip were to prop open the door and sign one of the shelves in ketchup, perhaps Charles Saatchi might be interested in paying a hundred grand for it.

The vegetable and fruit bins remind me of the drawers in a morgue. Within are the corpses of broccoli and apples and a bit of shriveled gray flesh that may have been an orange. Beneath the dead produce lie the remains of the remains, liquefied and permanently stuck to the plastic drawer.

When I open the freezer, jammed with tightly wrapped plastic bundles and Styrofoam take-out containers, Cullen suggests we call someone from Clemson's archaeology department. There is a package, unidentified, dated October 4, 1980. Everything is covered in a half inch layer of ice-hair. On five parcels, spanning the nineties, my father has printed "shrimp tails."

And soup. Flip loves soup. Many times he's called me to brag that he had created the definitive minestrone or gazpacho. The freezer contains the leftovers of every soup he ever made.

The rest of the house is the same, without the freezer burn.

I could order a Dumpster. I could put on my Hazmat suit, arm myself with an ice pick and a blowtorch, and return my father's house to habitability. But I can't do it without his approval, and he doesn't seem ready to let his sons take over. If I knew I'd be here for months, I'd take him on. But as it is, I have no idea whether it's a fight worth having.

I settle on a compromise. The rest of the house can remain mired in grime. But the refrigerator is mine.

Now that Cullen is here there's someone to sit with Flip while I go food shopping. And when I get back I intend to trash the deadest of the dead produce, and at least two packages of shrimp tails.

I drive my father's car five minutes to the local Bi-Lo grocery store. The building is relentlessly air-conditioned. The aisles are wide enough for those who prefer not to leave the safety of their SUVs while they shop. Two block-long aisles are stocked with orange Clemson gear. I would not have thought anyone would require a travel-ready infant changing station covered with paw prints.

I sit at an in-store Starbucks and drink iced coffee. Then I shop. Flip's long-standing interest in food has narrowed. Now he will eat only small pieces of bread, three types of Campbell's soup, and fruit-flavored Jell-O. I buy lots of each. And then I fill my cart with stuff for Cullen and me: cold cuts, fruit, a broiled chicken, salad fixings, cereal.

The situation at the checkout counter is unfamiliar to me. I stand around for a few moments, wondering when a cashier might appear. Finally a shopper comes up behind me and says I have to do it myself. I'm supposed to scan the bar codes and weigh the veggies and so forth. At first I think she is joking. I smile. She does not. She looks impatient, like she might run me over with her cart. I make a few attempts at running a salami over the scanner. Each time the machine barks at me.

"You have to give it your credit card," the woman behind me says.

"Ah, I see. Thank you. Does the machine say 'paper or plastic'?" I ask.

She stares at me blankly.

I insert my credit card and withdraw it. The machine lights up and welcomes me and squawks helpful instructions. I try again with the salami, and this time it beeps and registers a price. It's quite exciting, actually.

The house is quiet when I return. My brother and father are napping. I put away the groceries, throwing out only what is absolutely necessary to make room for the new stuff. But while the rotten squash and rock hard cheese and ancient chicken soup deserve to go, I feel extremely uncomfortable taking charge, even in this small way.

Why *should* he clean out the refrigerator or clean the bathtub? Who am I to fly in from California and decide that he doesn't need fourteen-year-old lamb bones?

In the afternoon, Flip is up, and we're watching television. I say I'm going to pee. I pass the guest bathroom and walk into my dad's room. A vanity is strewn with medicine. He has five bottles of OxyContin, a powerful pain drug, in varying doses spread around the sink. Two have no caps. I count eleven different prescription drugs in containers of all shapes and sizes crowded in among laxatives and over-the-counter pain meds and cough syrup and vitamins. It's total chaos. There's no way he has any clue what he's taking or when.

I sit on his bed, as I have done before. But this time I pull back the blankets. A wave of urine odor hits me.

Death is unfathomable. Although he wets the bed and is slow and has no appetite, I still have a father. The notion that sometime soon I'll never hear his live voice again, or smell him, or watch him walk across a room, is just that—an idea, an abstraction. I know he will die, but I don't have any idea what that means or how I can expect to feel when it happens.

# chapter twenty-three

# Brothers

FLIP LOOKS MUCH THE SAME as when I arrived a week ago—hunched over, sluggish getting off the couch, skin and bones except for his still protruding stomach. He sleeps twenty hours a day. He eats next to nothing. He gets more calories from his meds than from the half-bites of Jell-O and white toast he takes at meals.

But he doesn't seem to be getting much worse, either.

The phone rings incessantly. Flip won't talk to anyone, but I can see the interest pleases him. He particularly enjoys it when we report, from a call or a get-well card, that one of his Christian friends is praying for him.

"Now I'm really in trouble," he says.

There is one disturbing change, though: For the first time in his life my father has very little to say.

Jane arrived the past evening. Cullen and I sit in the living room catching up with our stepmother. Flip is silent. He watches us. It is difficult to explain how weird it is to be in my father's presence and not have him speaking, interrupting, opining, bullshitting. When he's not being directly addressed, and sometimes when he is, he seems elsewhere.

I ask him if he is looking forward to seeing his brother and nephew who are arriving the next day.

"I wish you'd tell them not to come."

"They flew from California," Jane says. "You don't have to spend a lot of time."

"I don't know why everyone wants to come to see me," Flip says. "I was very happy here by myself before you all started showing up."

We are all still for a minute.

"People who love you are worried and they want to be with you," I say.

He says nothing for a moment and then begins to cry.

"Don't they know how hard it is for me?"


When Flip was born, his parents named him Alfred. They pronounced their last name Schaffer, with a long *a*, like the beer.

In junior high school he took German. The teacher told him he was pronouncing his surname incorrectly. There is no *e* in the name, so it ought to be said with the short *a*, to rhyme with *gaffer*. From then on, Flip parted ways with the rest of his family, employing the German pronunciation.

In high school Alfred's friends started to call him Flip. He disliked his given name and was glad to be called anything else. The nickname was either because of my father's manner of shooting free throws, in which he bent over and flipped the ball in, underhanded, from between his legs, or after a saxophonist he and his friends admired named Flip Phillips.

As with much of my father's history, he had two stories about how the nickname came about; he told both stories with utter conviction at different times, and refused to concede, when he was telling one version, that any other existed.

Around the time my parents were married Flip began to use the name Alan.

So Alfred Schaffer (with the long *a*), became Flip Schaffer (like *gaffer*), who became Alan Schaffer.

When I was growing up, I knew my father had an older brother, Frank. Frank had several sons, though I was never clear just how many. Frank was supposed to be quite successful in business. He lived close to Flip's father, Louis, in Los Angeles. Over the years I saw my grandfather occasionally. I never saw Frank or my cousins. A few times I asked Flip why he didn't speak to his brother. He said they had a falling-out. Or he said they had nothing in common. Or he said they had nothing to say to each other. Or he said it was because they lived so far apart.

At the age of forty-four, Alan Schaffer left his family in New York, where he and his brother had been born and raised, and moved to the rural South. He married a southerner. He stopped writing fiction. Later, he destroyed all his writings. He smoked three packs of cigarettes a day for forty years.

When I see my father break down at the prospect of saying good-bye to his brother, it hits me that all of these circumstances are part of a single endeavor. Flip has spent his whole life dodging or escaping or leaving or breaking up with or destroying or killing anybody and anything that reminds him of him, including him.

But as with so much about my father, what is true—that Flip couldn't bear to be Flip, that he ran and ran from himself—is also not true. Without warning, in his fifties, he stopped smoking. He abandoned his children, but later he made a considerable though not always successful effort to be a good father. He married Jane and he stayed married. And, in the decade before he became ill, Flip and Frank became brothers again. They traveled together. They visited frequently. My father offered no explanation for the reunion.

Around the time he turned seventy, Flip shaved the closely cropped beard he'd worn my whole life. He left only a mustache. The change did not suit him. His jowls had jowls. The beard hid the loose flesh. He always said shaving was barbaric. The new look aged him. When I asked about it he said he just felt like a change.

But when he sent me a photo from a trip he took with my uncle, I understood immediately why the beard had disappeared. In the picture the two are standing in front of a bus wearing matching caps. Although my uncle is far thinner than Flip, he too has a fleshy face, and a mustache. They look like twins.

Frank and his son arrive the next morning. The visit is uneventful. Frank talks about his latest travels. My cousin describes the plans for remodeling his new house. My dad sits with us for half an hour, which is good for him these days. He says almost nothing. Eventually he rests his hand on my leg and indicates he's had it. I help him up. He hugs his brother and nephew, too exhausted to cry, I think. Then I walk him to his room.

\* \* \*

That afternoon Flip and Cullen and Jane sit in the living room watching a videotape made years ago of my dad and Frank touring the Upper East Side neighborhood where they grew up. I'm mixing a challah dough. The kitchen is open to the living room so I can see the action on the TV.

Challah, a traditional Jewish bread consumed particularly on the Sabbath and holidays, is basically bread that wants to be cake. The recipe looks very much like a straight dough baguette, except for the addition of extra fat, usually in the form of butter or oil, and eggs. In religious families the baker separates an olive-size piece of the dough and bakes it apart from the braided main loaf. After the challah emerges the baker burns the small section of bread to symbolize the destruction of the second temple.

Although I am not a religious person, this tradition appeals to me. When I bake challah at home I hold back a small piece of dough and feed it to my dog, who is from Israel. I am not so sure about Ginger's provenance, so I decide in this case to bake the loaf in one piece.

The videotape of Flip and Frank is hilarious for reasons that have nothing to do with its subject. Frank owns the video camera. The cameraman, who is unidentified, but I believe to be one of Frank's sons, seems not to grasp the basic rules of cinematography. Several times my father points to and starts talking about a building or a store across the street. The cameraman swings around so that I have the feeling I'm on a merry-go-round operated by a person who has had way too much coffee. At one point, without warning, the lens dives toward the pavement and I have the momentary urge to stick my hands out to brace a fall.

The usual film has one director. This one has three—Frank,

Flip, and Jane, who follows the action from outside the frame. Jane feels the narrators should speak up. Frank assures her the camera will pick up the sound. Flip wants to walk one way; the others head in the opposite direction. Frank interrupts the action repeatedly to give the cameraman operating instructions. Without warning the picture plunges to the left, like the view from the cockpit of a fighter that has just taken a direct hit.

Between jerks the camera freezes on my dad's face, and momentarily he looks like he's been caught molesting a sheep.

"Wait a minute, wait a minute," Frank says, while someone walks through the action.

Flip, perturbed, says, "Can't you see we're shooting a film here?"

Frank is the older brother. But this does not prevent my father from cutting him off at every opportunity, correcting perceived mistakes, and generally behaving as if Frank was his not very bright assistant. Several times Frank tries to get the cameraman to shut down while they move elsewhere, but Flip just goes on talking.

He says they went to Jewish school every afternoon: "The rabbis were all over ninety-five and their method of teaching was to beat the shit out of you." His bar mitzvah was at dawn. There was no party. He got a pen.

"It was a hard life," Frank says, describing how, after their mother died, he and Flip used to join their father at the store in the evening for dinner. "We never got any of the little luxuries. I never really got a gift."

"You got a bike," my father reminds him.

"Sure," Frank says, smiling impishly, "but it was a *stolen* bike."

Their elementary school, P.S. 70, was built in the 1860s. A teacher named Mrs. Freedman punished wayward students by kicking them with her wooden leg.

"Remember Mrs. Christie?" Frank says.

"Oh," Flip says, "Mrs. Christie. Sixth grade. Vicious teacher. Everyone hated her."

"She sat everybody in terms of their ability, from dumb to smart," Frank says.

"There was a wonderful kindergarten teacher," Flip says. "Every day we would walk around the neighborhood. Even though our parents had stores on the block we weren't allowed to say hello."

"True," Frank adds. "And the reason she walked was she knew the kids' parents had stores and as she went by she got free merchandise."

Flip—one of the few Jews in the school, who would later have a job writing columns for a socialist newspaper, who told me in New York that he still considered himself a communist—won the Daughters of the American Revolution award for good citizenship.

"Tony Curtis lived down the block," Frank says. Flip looks doubtful. "Sure, Bernie Schwartz. He lived on Seventy-fourth Street. His father had a tailor shop."

The brothers agree that their father was a notorious penny-pincher. Louis gave Flip an envelope at his wedding to Cookie. He told the newlyweds it had originally contained a hundred dollars. But he had to deduct the cost of his tuxedo and the cab fare. So the net gift was sixty-two dollars and change.

After the walking tour, the film continues later in the day in a hotel room. Flip and Frank sit close to each other in armchairs. The camera, now, is on a tripod. They talk about their lives together, growing up in Yorkville.

I put the challah dough to rest and sit next to Flip in the living room. He studies the screen closely, with a dubious look on his face.

After listening for a while, and without the slightest irony, Flip says, "Those guys have no idea what they're talking about."


Jane has a class to teach the next day, so she leaves for Atlanta in the early evening.

In the morning Cullen packs his things and carries them out to his car. Flip is on the couch. I'm in the kitchen cleaning up after breakfast. Cullen comes in from outside and crouches on the floor in front of Flip.

I'm suddenly horrified that he's leaving me alone with my father. I'm sure the only reason I've survived the past few days—taking over my dad's medication regimen, meeting with the Hospice lady, sneaking pads into my dad's bed to soak up the urine, sitting in this house at the end of the road to nowhere while Flip sleeps away what remains of his life—is because my older brother has been here with me. I have never loved someone this much or needed someone more.

Cullen says, "I'm going now."

Flip must have seen him carrying his stuff out to the car, but he looks shocked, upset.

Cullen puts his arm around Flip, who says, "I guess it's hard for you to see me this way."

I walk into the living room and sit on the floor facing them.

"That's not hard," Cullen says. "What's hard is that I wish you could go on being my father forever."

"I know I haven't always been the best father."

"You tried, though."

"You tried, too," Flip says.

I'm sobbing. But they are not.

"Mostly people try and they fail," Cullen says. "But we *did* it. We worked it out."

With that Flip seems to fade out. Cullen hugs him, then me, then he leaves.

# chapter twenty-four

# Benzos

I T'S ELEVEN P.M. and I'm in Flip's office battling his computer. The computer is winning. I have to get a brief to San
Francisco in time for a morning filing. I get as far as attaching
the file to an e-mail message and hitting the send button.
Then the screen freezes. Although Flip could easily afford a
decent machine, he has chosen a cheapo, off-brand model. I
wonder if he bought the thing just so it would crash regularly, giving him an excuse to call me and complain about
what a screwed-up computer he has. The first thing I plan to
do when my father dies is to take the machine up to the roof
and drop it off.

I hear something collapse in Flip's room. I rush in to find
him parked in the master bathroom. He seems to be trying to
urinate. His robe is open. He is holding his penis and staring
down. I tiptoe in, hoping not to frighten him. He doesn't
seem to notice that a two-foot-long shelf above the tank has
fallen and its contents—a hairbrush, a roll of toilet paper, a
magazine, and a box of Q-tips—are now in the toilet. I put
my hand on his shoulder. He doesn't react.

"You all right, Pop?"

"Whaaat?"

He remains statuesque, head down, right hand aiming, left hand on his waist.

"I heard the stuff fall."

No response.

"Whaaat?" He says, again, louder than necessary. His tone suggests that just as soon as he's done emptying his bladder he plans to strangle me.

"You think I should take that stuff out of the toilet?"

He doesn't answer. I wait with him for several minutes, rubbing his shoulders. He mumbles off and on, but I can't make out what he's saying. Finally he turns around and takes a step toward his bedroom.

He snaps out of his half-sleep, and says, worriedly, "What's going on? What's happening?"

He glances around and sees that he's pushed the shelf above the toilet off its brackets and that the brush and other things have fallen into the bowl, which is filled with urine.

"For Christ's sake. What the hell is wrong with me?"

"Don't worry. I'll clean it up."

My words don't calm him. He starts to kneel down and crumples onto the floor.

"This is just ridiculous," he says.

"Will you please forget about it? Let's just get you to bed."

"Make sure you throw those things out," he says, pointing to the bowl.

A few hours earlier I'd given him an Ativan, a type of muscle relaxant, a benzodiazepine, like Valium. Most of the drugs on my dad's list are alien to me. But I grew up with a self-medicating shrink. Benzos I know.

I assume Flip's on the Ativan so he'll sleep through the night. He's more agitated now than I've seen him. I think it's probably the cancer, clawing into his brain, confusing him. The Ativan must not be working, or it's wearing off. So I figure there's no harm in giving him another, to zonk him out and get him, and me, some rest.

There were some advantages to being raised by Cookie. For example, at a relatively young age, I learned to appreciate the importance of prescription drugs in a well-lived life.

Once, I emptied two mirrored cabinets in Cookie's bathroom of thirty prescription bottles and spread them out on the slate floor. I removed a pill from each container and strung a pharmaceutical train from the vanity to the tub. Gelcaps started to melt in drops of water. The rust-colored, hard plastic bottles fascinated me as much as their contents—the mysterious language on the labels, warnings and directions. And on each one my mother's name: Dr. Schaffer. Other people's mothers baked and took them for field trips and fixed their zippers when they stuck. My mother ordered her drugs over the phone and had them delivered.

Cookie had it all. Painkillers of various makes and models for her muscle aches and backaches. Tubs of antibiotics. Pills to stop you up and pills to unstop you. Tablets to put you out and tablets to wake you up. Meds for colds and allergies and fevers. And many others I could not identify, some of which were for her depression.

Long before Prozac, Cookie tried to medicate herself out of her misery. I always knew she was on some new psych medication when her diet changed. For one drug she had to give up her beloved Camembert, for another the red wine disappeared. As far as I could tell, none of it helped.

Once I let my friend Josh, whose parents were psychiatrists, and who was more pharmaceutically conversant then I was, survey Cookie's stash. He informed me that some of the pills were the kind people took for fun—particularly the little blue ones called Valium. I was thirteen when I learned the word *benzodiazepine*. My mother's Valium bottle was about the size of a pint of ice cream.

We went to Josh's house, where he had his own floor. We swallowed the pills. I had two.

I wasn't awake for more than twenty minutes, and then I slept straight through the night. Josh had to call Cookie to say I was sleeping over. I remember thinking, before I nodded off, that my lower lip had lost all its muscle tone and was hanging down around my neck. I remember feeling very happy and swearing that when I sobered up I'd tell my mother she should be taking more of these.

I'd actually like to give Flip *several* Ativan, to put him out for a couple of days while I get some rest. I don't think I'd actually kill him that way.

But anyway it's hard enough to persuade him to swallow the one pill. The more he cedes control of his care and feeding to me, the more paranoid he becomes. He wants to know why he has to take an Ativan when he took one earlier. I tell him it'll help him sleep. He says he doesn't need it to sleep. I tell him I'm going to take one myself. He gives me a look that says, *Fine, whatever you want. I don't have the energy to argue.* He swallows the pill and flops into bed. Within thirty seconds I hear his irregular gasps and grunts.

I feel very pleased with myself. Flip was agitated. It's hard watching him fail, but at least I can make his dying days more comfortable.

I do not brush my teeth. I do not read. I kill the lights in my room, strip off my clothes, and fall out. In what seems like four seconds, but is actually four hours, I hear mayhem in the kitchen. I flip on the light and run down the hallway. My father, recently unable to get himself off the couch without help, has managed to drag a twenty-pound tub of dog food across the house and is emptying it onto the kitchen floor, handful by handful. He mumbles to himself and, kicking the kibble in every direction, paces three steps one way and three steps another. He is like a pinball at the mercy of invisible bumpers.

I can't make out a word he's saying. But it's very clear he has an agenda, and that something is upsetting him.

I push the tub of dog food out of the way and sweep most of the kibble aside with my foot. Then I push him up against the kitchen counter. He struggles to get away.

"What's wrong?" I say, applying more pressure, pinning him with my body.

From him, gibberish and rubbish and then, very clearly, "Ginger."

"What about Ginger? She's fine."

"I gotta walk her."

He becomes increasingly frantic while I restrain him, so I let go. He makes for the door at a surprising pace. I now understand how mothers of three-year-olds can lose their children in an instant. Even the very short or very sick can move quickly, at least in short bursts. I'm on his tail but he beats me to the door and gets it halfway open. I lean on it.

"I'll walk her in the morning. Please go back to bed."

He's crazed, panting and sweating.

He pulls at the door. I give up.

"You know what, Pop. If you want to walk Ginger at four thirty in the morning, who the hell am I to stop you. I could actually use some air."

Not that there's any air outside in August in South Carolina. I guide him down the path toward Ginger's house. By the time we're halfway across the yard the dog emerges, confused I suppose, but apparently pleased to sacrifice a little shut-eye for an after-hours stroll with the boss. She stands there, waiting to be leashed.

Did I mention that Flip is stark naked?

There is no evidence of human activity on the cul-de-sac. It's still so hot out that clothes are hardly necessary. And the mosquitoes seem to be sleeping.

His naked, middle-of-the-night dog walk seems to be proof that the cancer has invaded my father's brain and that he is going to die tonight, or shortly. I consider giving him another Ativan, but it's an argument I'd rather not have at four thirty a.m.

The walk is rather pleasant, and mercifully short, just to the end of the driveway and back to Ginger's house. Flip says nothing, but it seems to calm him. After, he lets me guide him into the house and back to bed.

I grab a blanket and pillow and wedge myself into the doorway of my father's room. The floor is covered with just a thin layer of matted carpet. But there's no way I'm sleeping in my bed tonight. If he makes another run for it, I want to know.

I curl up on the floor and watch him sleep. And it hits me that all the things about Flip that once infuriated me—his lying, his arrogance, how when I immediately failed to grasp his point he became dismissive—are gone. He's still a pain in the ass, but now it's because he wants to walk the dog when I want to sleep, or won't let me clean up his messes.

He's so childlike that I've stopped thinking about how he failed me. The resentment I felt my whole life, and continued to cling to—even after he acknowledged how he hurt me by leaving, even after he described how he was haunted by guilt, even after he apologized—is gone. Now all I can think about is trying to put myself between Flip and his suffering and humiliation.

For the first time in my life, I'm not angry.

My mother and I declared a ceasefire in June of 1982. After spending four months at Flip's house in Clemson, I returned to New Rochelle just before my high school graduation. Neither of my parents bothered to show up, but I didn't mind. I'd already left home. I was just back for a two-month visit before going off to Cornell. I felt grown-up, no longer in need of parental approval or encouragement. I spent the day at the beach with two friends, got extremely drunk, and almost didn't make it back in time for the ceremony.

I got along quite well with Cookie that summer. We saw very little of each other, which helped. In return for housing and use of her car, I made her bed in the morning, ironed her clothing, shopped for food, and cleaned the house. By the time she got home from work I'd already left to go out with my friends.

Also, she was so horribly depressed that she lacked the energy to fight. She worked and slept and watched TV and smoked. Our conversations were like this:

I walked into the television room. She was on the couch with her knees tucked into her chest, wearing a worn blue velour bathrobe, an ashtray in one hand, a cigarette in the other. She slowly turned her head toward me.

"Hey, Mom."

"Hello."

"What's up?"

She shrugged.

"I'm going out with Josh."

She shrugged.

"You want me to pick up anything for your dinner?"

She shook her head.

She was too depressed to notice that, just as she had predicted, I was about to go off the deep end.

The dim, blank mood I lived in at my dad's house returned with me to New Rochelle. At the end of July I came home from a party. Cookie was away at a conference for the weekend. I went into her bathroom for her Valium. I was already drunk and I think, initially, I just wanted to sleep. I swallowed a pill. It was small. No chaser required.

I tipped over the bottle and a baby blue tide washed over my white Formica desk. Then it occurred to me that I didn't have to live in such pain. I had a choice. And I chose to die.

One by one, left hand, right hand, left, right, I plucked the pills from my desk and swallowed them. Then I went to my mother's liquor cabinet for a quart bottle of Smirnoff vodka. I took it to my room and drank as much of it as I could before passing out.

I did not die, as you may have gathered. That me is so remote that I cannot even be certain I wanted to die. Perhaps I was just trying to get some attention.

The only part of it I remember clearly is that once I started swallowing the pills I no longer felt like I was making a decision. It seemed as if someone else was feeding me and that I trusted that person to know what was best.

I wake Jen at five a.m. California time and tell her what happened with my dad. She says, kindly but firmly, that I should stop pretending to be a doctor. I don't have any idea what I'm doing. She explains that because Flip's kidneys aren't functioning properly, he can't metabolize the Ativan. He shouldn't be on the stuff at all. He's not demented, she says. It was the drugs. A day off the benzos and he should be back to normal.

# chapter twenty-five

# Estates of Mind

H E *IS* CALMER the next day, less befuddled. And he has an agenda.

Shortly after Flip learned that he had a terminal illness he called to discuss his affairs. He explained that he had, for the most part, left his small estate to Jane. He'd made small bequests of money or prized objects to each of his children. I asked him whether he had a will, and he assured me he did. I asked whether he had signed documents making clear how he wants us to proceed should he become incapacitated. He said he did.

Since then, Flip and I have had this exact conversation several hundred times.

So now, having told me again and again over the past three years that his affairs are in order, Flip leads me into his office to show me that his affairs are in order. I sit at his desk, ready to take notes. Dressed in his maroon bathrobe he kneels next to a metal filing cabinet. His pace in all things now is lethargic. His blinks are heavy and sluggish. He pulls out the drawer as if it weighed a thousand pounds. He fingers the files and, with much effort, withdraws one thick with documents. He opens it and hands me his will. I pretend to read it.

Then he runs through a variety of bank and brokerage accounts, mortgages, insurance policies, credit cards, and pensions. I take a few notes. He explains that I'll have to help Jane with these matters when he dies. I say I won't let him down.

In August of 1996 I was living with two friends in a house in San Francisco. The phone rang at ten in the morning. A housemate answered. It was Cullen on the line, she said.

"Hey, Cul," I said, cheerfully.

"Mom's dead."

The receiver was on my left ear. I put my index finger into my right ear. Somehow this made the conversation more private. Then I collapsed over a counter and sobbed into the kitchen sink. I turned on the cold water and ran it over my hands and splashed it up into my face. I got back on the phone and said I'd get a flight to New York the next morning.

Flip came to New York, to support us, he said. For the few days he was there he seemed not sure what to do with himself, not even sure what to feel. What is the proper role of a long-ex husband in such circumstances? He expressed sadness at how unhappy Cookie was, but I suppose in private he may have patted himself on the back for having the smarts to get away before she destroyed him. I never saw him cry.

At the memorial service, in Cookie's townhouse, we were the focus of attention. Flip stood at the end of the long living room with cathedral ceilings, looking out over the lake behind the house. He chatted with members of my family he hadn't seen in twenty-five years. He ate bagels and lox and potato salad. Probably he was sorry there were no bialys, but he didn't mention it.

I went to him when I'd had enough of superficially sad conversations with people I didn't know or care much about. I sat with him and said I was sad, but I was also relieved.

"Finally these people have no choice but to believe me," I said. "For my whole life I've been trying to tell everyone how crazy she was, that it wasn't me. Now I have some tangible evidence to hold up, to prove that my mother was nuts."

"I always believed you," he said.

"That may be," I said. "But you didn't do anything about it."

I was ready to go at it with him, right there in the middle of my mother's living room. But he didn't take the bait. He just patted my knee three times and escaped to the bathroom.

For a time it seemed as if Cookie hadn't made any parting remarks, which would have been extremely surprising. Eventually we discovered a note. The handwriting was legible, which means she wrote it before the bottle of barbiturates took effect. It also means she really wanted us to read it, because my mother had notoriously lousy script. At the close of the note she wrote, *I realize that this will affect each of you differently and I hope you will be supportive to one another.* She signed it, *Your Mother.*

It was a nice sentiment. It would have been more meaningful had she not done everything in her power to ensure that precisely the opposite would happen. Cookie was not content with having had a miserable life and dying on purpose. She wanted the fighting to go on after she was gone. So she divided her estate in a manner designed to hurt and infuriate and divide her children.

A few days after she died my three siblings and I sat in a lawyer's office near Wall Street. The lawyer read Cookie's will. Essentially, my sister, Wendy, got everything.

When we left the office we began a discussion about the will, and whether we—or more accurately Wendy—would accept its terms. We sat around my sister's small apartment in lower Manhattan discussing and then arguing over what Cookie had done, and what we could do to remedy the situation. Wendy said then, and again and again over the next year, that she felt obligated to respect my mother's wishes. I said then, and repeated in our many conversations about the will that followed, that our mother was mentally ill, and that her point in excluding her sons from the estate was to express her anger at men in general, not at us in particular. The reasonable thing to do, I said, was to acknowledge my mother's problems, and split the money four ways, or give it all away. The one thing we *shouldn't* do was to respect what she had done, which was designed to drive us apart.

Wendy took the cash. I can't really blame her. It was more than two million dollars. I might have done the same thing. But I decided that if she wouldn't acknowledge how destructive my mother had been, then I could do without such a sister. We haven't spoken since.


Flip was an enthusiastic amateur woodworker. After more than a week at my dad's, I've noticed two things about his homemade furniture, which litters the house. First, it looks pretty good, like the person who made it knows something about carpentry.

And second, each piece has at least one glaring defect. At

first glance, a varnished box on Flip's desk appears to be a nice example of a varnished box, its ends joined together with elegant dovetails. Turn the box around, though, and you find that some of the dovetails look more pounded and mashed than joined. And if you look closely, the box is really a parallelogram, not a rectangle. Same for the desk with the drawer that won't open unless you pull to the left, and the end table with the sawed-off corner.

When Flip goes to sleep and I delve a little deeper into his papers, I learn that precisely these observations apply to his financial affairs. On the surface, things look pretty good. He has meticulously labeled his files and separated out important documents. He has organized his bills into categories. But like the chair with the one slightly-too-long leg, in almost every case there is a serious hitch.

Flip was understating the case when he assured me that he has a will. In fact, Flip has several wills, which are the same in all but two or three very important ways. Which might not be a problem if the will with the most recent date, which contains the terms he seems most committed to, was signed.

Everything is more complicated than it has to be. The brokerage account he wants to give the kids is going to Jane. The durable power of attorney and healthcare proxy were executed in Georgia, making them, possibly, worthless in South Carolina. The bills are in folders, but it's impossible to know what has been paid. Checks are missing. The mortgage has not been paid for two months. A manila folder contains small slips of white paper with Flip's incomprehensible scribblings, which may or may not contain critical data about stock sales and transfers between accounts.

Perhaps most bizarre, my father's various wills establish a trust to benefit his wife, which, after her death, would be distributed to his children. This is the sort of thing people do, so on its face the trust makes sense. But Flip has gone to great lengths to make sure Jane gets all his money and stocks and pension immediately upon his death. The trust will be costly and time-consuming to set up, and it's totally pointless.

There's nothing to do about any of it. I have no intention of informing my father that he's bungled things in all sorts of creative ways. Even if I were to try to correct the problems, I'd have to get him to sign documents in a mental state that might not qualify as sound in a South Carolina court.

chapter twenty-six

# One in a Row

I'M A PRISONER, alone with Flip. Each day he gets sicker, less able to fend for himself. But I like it.

I've spent plenty of time during my nearly four decades in a state of unreserved gloom, often for no good reason at all. Now, my father is dying and I'm alone and I'm bored out of my mind. Still, I'm not depressed. I'm not even sad. I'm as content as I have ever been.

Once I took a cab to the top of a nineteen-thousand-foot volcano in Ecuador. The driver waited while, for an hour, I sat outside on the ground, freezing my ass off. I was totally unprepared for the weather, dressed in thin pants and a T-shirt. A squall sliced across the barren rock at the top of the mountain and when it reached me it felt like a cat was tearing at my face. But I felt happy then, in extremis. The pain was a reminder of how sublime life really is. Perhaps it's the same with Flip. Or perhaps I just like being in charge of my father. Or maybe I'm in denial.

When he gets out of bed in the morning I make toast. He takes a few bites and has a quarter cup of tea. After, he sits on the couch sucking tanked oxygen into his nose, watching, or, more accurately, staring at the television. I haven't seen him pick up a book since I arrived. We say very little. I report on who has called or written. I relate various news: The social worker is coming Thursday to qualify him for Hospice care; the doctor says he should up the pain meds whenever he likes; I'm taking money out of his checking account to cover some household expenses; Jen and Guthrie will arrive in the next few days. Then he goes to bed.

At lunch, I make Campbell's chicken and rice soup. He has a few spoonfuls. I help him over to the couch and return with a box of photographs. I remove the pictures one at a time. Mostly he says nothing. Once or twice he names a relative or friend.

I take out a picture of a gravestone. At the top is Hebrew lettering. Below that it reads, "Elsie Schaffer, Died, August 28, 1945. Age 40 Years." This is the first time in my life I have seen documentary evidence of Flip's mother. I did not know her name or when she died or how old she had been. My dad never mentioned her, and when we asked him, he always said he didn't remember. Flip doesn't react to the picture. He looks at it for a moment and sets it aside.

Later I find pictures from my parents' wedding. In one, Cookie's father is helping her out of a black stretch limo. She is seventeen years old. She is wearing a white lace gown and a long veil and white shoes. She looks optimistic. I have a hard time seeing the Cookie I knew in the pictures.

"You can't tell she was miserable," I say. "You wouldn't think this person had recently been in a mental hospital."

"She only told me the day we got married."

"Really?"

"I asked her why she didn't say anything before. She said she was afraid I'd leave her."

"Did she try to kill herself? Is that why she went into the institution?"

"Not that I know of. The doctors thought she should get away from her mother." Long pause. "She stayed friends with a guy from the institution. He was an Orthodox Jew who sold hams."

I ask about a photograph of an attractive, curvy woman that looks like it was taken in the forties or fifties.

"That's my wife," he says.

Flip told us he was married before Cookie, but until this moment I always assumed it was one of his inventions.

"Maybe we should nail this down, if you don't mind," I say.

"I don't mind."

"How many times were you married?"

"Three."

"Okay, three. You're sure."

"I'm sure."

"Because it seems to me for a long time it was four," I say.

"No. Three."

"So, Jane is three, and mom was two. And one?"

I point to the picture.

"Nancy Salo," he says.

"And you met where?"

"In the movement. We were involved in politics."

"What was she like?"

"Tall and beautiful," he says. "She was a dancer."

"Like a ballet dancer."

"In a chorus line. At the Copacabana."

"You married a dancer from the Copacabana?"

"Yeah."

"Seriously."

"Why would I lie?"

Any satisfactory answer to this question is bound to insult my father, so I make no attempt.

"Jewish?" I say.

"No. Finnish."

I laugh, hard. Flip tries not to smile, but he can't help himself.

Later he falls asleep on the living room couch, which means I can't watch television or work in the kitchen. So I take the opportunity to change his sheets and pee pad and give his bathroom a quick once over. I notice several boxes buried in the back of his overcrowded closet. I drag one into the hallway and open it. It is stuffed with yellowed, dusty files. In one, held together by a rusting paper clip, is what appears to be an early draft of *One in a Row,* the play that opened the night I was born, the play he assured me in New York, over and over again, he had destroyed.

I look further and find several more versions of the play. And reviews. And correspondence between Flip and his agents, and Flip and the producers, and Flip and his friends, all reflecting in minute detail the history of the production.

The other boxes are similarly swollen, with, as far as I can tell, everything my father wrote before he moved to South Carolina—plays, stories, novels, academic articles, an inch-thick folder of letters from Leon Arden.

I'm not mad. I'm delighted. I want to run out into the living room and hug him and say, "You lying bastard." But

I just sit there and thumb through the papers. I remove a bound copy of *One in a Row* and put it under my pillow in the guest room. I check on Flip. And then I return to his room and read what I can from the boxes until he wakes.

In the process, I learn a few interesting things about my father. For example, he won twelfth prize in the 1961 *Writer's Digest* short story contest, which earned him a Remington Premier Portable typewriter, which is also in the closet. He published a short story in the *Alfred Hitchcock Mystery Magazine* and one in a racy men's magazine called *Gent*. That story, "The Magic Derriere," is about an executive who hires a secretary who proves to be particularly handy. Specifically, when the executive pats or pinches the secretary's rear end, a five-dollar bill floats out of her skirt.

On a single page, undated, Flip writes the following:

About three weeks ago I woke up one morning and in that pleasant half-awake half-asleep time, reached down to my crotch and felt my balls. They were very big, very big indeed. All my adult life women have periodically said to me, "Boy, you got big balls," a point of rather childish pride with me. Thus, it was hardly accidental that I muttered to myself that morning, "Boy, you got big balls." Then, as I really awoke, I suddenly realized that while my balls are big, they're not that big, not nearly that big. Lying there, I felt them, and somehow sensed that they were indeed not big, but gigantic, and while I felt a mild sexual urge, the size of my balls did not correspond to the nature of the need. Pushing back the covers I looked down at my scrotum and realized quite how big my balls were. Leaping up I ran to the mirror where I could really see them and knew that I had developed into a freak overnight. First of all my balls were not really immense. That is, my left ball was normal, but my right ball was gigantic, huge, a legend in its own sac and all that.

The first right thought that came to mind, since I do smoke a lot, was cancer of the balls, a disease I believe I invented on the spot. I kept racking my brain trying to develop a link between smoking and the scrotum and, failing to develop any, I instantly came up with guilt. This was God's vengeance upon me. But for what? I have been leading a restricted life, no worse and no better than the life I have always led. What was I being punished for? Obviously, sexual excess. I remember shrugging at that for if my life is filled with sexual excesses I would hate to see the left or right ball of someone who has a normal sex life. Finally, after what seemed like hours of theological speculation, I did the only thing left to me: I called a doctor. Three hours later I was undressing in the office of the good surgeon Weiss. I took off my pants, took off my underwear, and subjected my scrotum to his scrutiny. "Boy," he said, shaking his head. "You got big balls." While this affirmed the opinions of some women I have known carnally, it was not what I was paying him for. He felt, he prodded, he squeezed (gently, gently), and finally made up his mind. I had an epidimitis, an inflammation of the scrotal liquid, the epidimis. Epidimitis is the singular form, the plural is epidimidides, who I believe is also responsible for some of the more vulgar Greek plays. Dr. Weiss prescribed an antibiotic and after about three weeks my balls are nearly normal but I still have a slight list to the right which will take months of occupational therapy to overcome. I told my psychoanalyst all this right after telling her how bitchy my wife has become and she asked me if I had ever heard the expression "she's got you by the balls," at which point I would have cracked up had it not been too painful.

It's thrilling, the thought that the thousands of pages in these tattered boxes might provide some clues as to who my father really is, what he thinks, what he's been hiding all these years beneath layers of fabrication and posturing and denial. And it's a window that won't close when the cancer finally beats him.

Later, I'm in the kitchen. Flip is sitting at the dining room table, staring at the opposite wall. My cell phone rings. It's my agent calling from New York. She has sold my first novel.

I sit with my dad and tell him the news. Tears begin to stream down his face.

He says, "I'm so glad I lived long enough to see this happen. This is the happiest day of my life."

And I believe him.

I've always fantasized that when I finally read *One in a Row,* I would discover that my father is a genius, and that I would dedicate myself to bringing his work to the public. I have a clear image of me pacing the back of the Public Theater in New York, hands jammed into suit pants pockets. When the crowd erupts at the first funny line, I remove my hands, cross my arms on my chest, and stop pacing. When the audience stands, cheering, at the end of the first act, my heart swells.

And when the people stomp their feet and clap raucously at the final curtain, I jog up to the stage and accept the ovation on Flip's behalf.

I can only read the play for the first time once. So it is with great hesitation that I crack open the dusty, faded blue cardboard cover of the manuscript. I lie in bed, propped up on my elbows, a night-light focused on the pages, like a spotlight on a soliloquizing actor.

chapter twenty-seven

# Angels

A FEW YEARS AGO, Flip and I had an argument on the subject of playwriting. I said my most moving experience in the theater had been a production of Tony Kushner's *Angels in America,* in San Francisco, in the midst of the AIDS crisis. Given that the epic drama received the Pulitzer Prize, two Tony Awards, two Drama Desk Awards, the Evening Standard Award, two Olivier Award nominations, the New York Critics Circle Award, and the Los Angeles Drama Critics Circle Award, I believed then, as I believe now, that I was on firm ground in suggesting that the play is, at least, pretty good.

My father, having written a few plays, and having had one produced three decades before to tepid reviews from the Rochester, New York, press, said I was wrong about *Angels.* Speaking as an expert of the form, he said the play was "just bad writing." His superciliousness infuriated me, but I let it go.

Sometime later Flip took me to see a comedy by the playwright *he* most admires, Moss Hart. It was a smart if slightly dated farce. I enjoyed it. And I tried, I really, really tried, not to say what I was thinking, which was that it couldn't hold a candle to *Angels*. His play was fun, mine was transcendent; his you forget in an hour, mine you remember on your deathbed. Anyway, I told him I enjoyed the play a great deal. I thanked him for the lovely evening. I was on my best behavior.

But the man simply couldn't hold his tongue.

It was the worst argument I ever had with my father. The more he tried to explain why he believed Hart could write a decent play, and Kushner could not, the more I wanted to assault him. His arrogance was appalling. I thought, *What the hell have you done in your life that gives you the right to render an opinion on the quality of Tony Kushner's toenail clippings?* I could hardly look at him after, finally, we agreed to disagree. But every time I saw him I remembered the superior, dismissive look on his face when he described one of the last century's great works of art as "a piece of unadulterated crap."

The next morning I drive up to the Greenville-Spartanburg Airport to fetch Jen. Flip is awake when we return. And in a stirring demonstration of my father's resolve, if not to live, then at least to stand up while greeting a beautiful woman, he meets us at the door. Jen has no idea how extraordinary this is. She hugs him. I prepare to catch him should he collapse. But he does not. Jen removes his glasses.

"Whaaat?" he says.

She cleans them with her shirt.

"How can you see a thing?"

She returns them.

"This is nice, but I gotta go lie down," he says, and disappears into his room.

Despite the grimy condition of the house, I've done very little tidying since I arrived. While Flip slept, I tried to earn some money working on law projects. Other than the kitchen, which I cleaned thoroughly in order to have space to bake, I've essentially left the house alone. Like my father, I'm bothered by clutter, but not really by filth.

Jen, though, is an enthusiastic scrubber and duster and mopper. I can't very well stand by while my wife cleans my dying father's house, so I join in. Later Flip emerges from his room. I'm standing on a chair, removing black sludge from the top of a light fixture. He leans against a counter and looks up at me. Jen is kneeling on a counter wiping down moldy molding.

"Oh Jesus," he says. "It's a holocaust of cleaning."

Had I been alone he would have ordered me to stop. He wouldn't even let me move his papers off the dining room table. But Jen's presence changes everything. Flip adores her. Perhaps this is so in part because, unlike the rest of his children, he never left her, so he feels no guilt.

"This place is disgusting, Alan," she says. "How can you live here?"

I hold my breath. I'll divorce her. If she makes him mad, I'll dump her like a load of moldy oranges.

He says, "Whatever you want to do is fine."

Later I'm on the deck sweeping while Jen scrapes muck off the windows. Flip appears behind the sliding glass door. He looks worried. He withdraws into the house. I walk inside. He is not there, but the front door is open. I walk out into the yard. He is making his way across the yard to his workshop with Ginger at his heels.

"Pop. What are you doing?"

He doesn't answer. I follow closely behind, but I don't think he knows I'm there. It takes him two minutes to walk thirty feet, get the key into the door, and open it. I watch from outside. He disappears for a moment and returns trailing a leaf blower. The thing must weigh sixty pounds and it takes every ounce of strength he has to drag it along. It gets stuck on the door jamb. I run over to him.

"Pop, you must be joking."

He is not pleased to see me.

"I'll do it," he says.

I get behind the machine and lift it just off the ground so he can pull it along almost effortlessly.

It takes us a while to reach the back deck. Flip insists on setting up the blower. He does not seem to know that he is emaciated and frail and on the verge of kicking off. He has every intention of running the debris off his deck himself.

I know he can't do it. I want to spare him the realization. But there's no way to do so without humiliating him anyway. He turns it on and the machine shrieks and the hose flaps uncontrollably around the deck. I lift the body of the blower.

"I'll hold it. You take the hose," I say.

"All right," he says. He blows for a few seconds, shouting instructions I can't hear. Then he hands over the hose and walks unsteadily into the house.

To qualify for Hospice, a social worker has to interview Flip and the family and check out the house, to make sure we're able to act as his primary caretakers. Now Jen's insistence that we clean the house seems yet another example of her wisdom. If the social worker had seen the house in its pre-Jen condition, I suppose she might have concluded we were trying to kill my father.

The social worker arrives in her small blue Toyota at two p.m. Ginger goes nuts, barking, growling, darting back and forth across the lawn. Guthrie, who arrived earlier in the day, and I go outside to see what's up. The social worker, a young African American woman, rolls down the passenger side window and declines, wisely, to get out of her car. I call the dog, who ignores me. I run after her and she runs away, toward the car. The social worker rolls up her window.

Finally we capture Ginger and put her in her house. Guthrie stands at the entrance, preventing the dog from mauling the social worker. The woman is still in her car. I walk over.

The car's window is still closed, so I half say, and half gesture, "It's fine. You're safe. She's just protecting the property." The woman rolls down her window.

"You'll be fine now," I say. "Really. We've got her tied up."

Ginger barks incessantly as the woman warily makes her way up Flip's driveway and into the house. Guthrie and I follow. We ask her to sit down and offer her a soda.

Ginger gets loose and charges full-bore toward the house and smacks into the front door, snarling and growling. The social worker gets off the couch and recedes into the kitchen. Guthrie runs outside to tie up the dog.

Flip—who dedicated much of his career at Clemson to recruiting and encouraging and supporting and advocating for African American students; who, though he was no musician, was for years the faculty adviser to the University's Black Gospel Choir; who had no tolerance for bigotry of any kind—turns to the social worker and says, "Ginger doesn't like Black people."

The woman is wild-eyed, on the verge of fleeing.

I explain that he means the dog seems to be *afraid* of Black people. I tell her about my dad's work on behalf of Black students at Clemson. I say far too much, apparently, because the social worker looks more, not less terrified.

After a brief interview and tour of the house she leaves. We escort her out the back door, and around the side of the house, hoping Ginger will not notice. We have no such luck.

I'm now very concerned the social worker is going to file a negative report, perhaps advising that my father's care be taken over by the local sheriff and that the rest of us be run out of the state.

It's one a.m. I'm wide-awake and stuck in my dad's office because a sleeping body occupies every other room in the house. I click around the directories on my dad's computer and find one that's labeled *stuff*. In it is a single Microsoft Word file called *Pop.doc.*

My father still has a heartbeat. I have no right to look at what he's written. I know this. I have no defense. I open it because I can and because I'm curious and because I'm bored. But I feel better when, after opening the file, I see the following at the top of the page: *For my sons, my daughter, my nephews, their spouses, their children, and anyone else who's interested.*

It is a ten-page reminiscence. He talks about growing up in Yorkville. He describes returning to the apartment he shared with his father one day to discover that a woman and her two children had moved in. He ran to his father's store. Louis said, "That's Esther. We got married this morning." He repeats stories I've been hearing my whole life—about the teacher with the wooden leg, about his boyhood pal Eddie Fizieri, whose father had a shoe repair shop.

But it is the first paragraph of the document that is most striking:

> I used to tell people that my mother died when I was young. I said I didn't remember much about her. The truth is, I remember very well. I was fourteen going on fifteen. I remember her being an invalid, in and out of hospitals and nursing homes. I remember not being unhappy when she died. In fact I spent much of my private time as a child wishing she were dead. When she died I considered it a blessing for the family, but I also felt responsible because of my death wish for her, a burden I carried into adulthood.

If I were to suggest to my father that his attitude toward *Angels in America* has to do with his own experience, he'd tell me I was out of my mind. And to a point, I have to take him at his word when he says he dislikes the play. It's not for everyone. It's tough going, not funny, mostly, and fantastical in parts.

Still, reading my father's confession, it's impossible not to wonder if he loathes *Angels* because it kicks up overwhelming feelings of guilt. In one of the drama's central stories, a character, Louis (which also happens to be my grandfather's name), deserts his dying lover, Prior, and thereafter is tormented by remorse. And one of the main questions *Angels* raises is whether Prior should forgive Louis, and, indeed, whether redemption is even possible in the case of such abandonment.

The same question applies to Flip's life.

He left his children knowing Cookie couldn't manage. And, as he told me in New York, he's been haunted by remorse ever since.

And now I know he wished his mother dead. He admits he was not unhappy when she died. And he suffered for the rest of his life with the shame of believing that he was responsible, that he killed her.

I suppose for my father the play is simply too much to bear.

# chapter twenty-eight

# The Last Bialy

O N  T H E  M O R N I N G of my thirty-ninth birthday I decide to attempt my first batch of bialys. I find a recipe on the Web and gather the ingredients in the kitchen.

Flip walks into the dining room and sits. I want him to acknowledge the day. I don't expect it, though. He seems increasingly unattached to what's happening on Earth.

After a few minutes he says, "Happy birthday, Sonny."

I hug him and return to the kitchen.

For as long as I have known him, Flip has clutched his nose once or twice each day with his right hand, squeezed together his nostrils, and noisily said, "HONK," as if he were describing, to a four-year-old, the sound a truck or goose makes. He claims this clears his sinuses.

While I'm dicing onions for the topping that sits in the middle of each bialy, he "HONKS." I haven't heard him "HONK" since I've been in Clemson. I take it as a sign that he is rallying, perhaps even because it's my birthday.

I tear open a packet of freeze-dried yeast—the best I can do in Clemson—and measure out the flours. Then I carry the large bowl into the dining room and knead next to him. He watches intently as the glutens form and the mush becomes dough. I gather the kneaded dough into a ball and present it to him.

He smells it and pokes it with his thumb.

"Pretty good," he says.

"I'm worried it'll rise too fast. It's so humid here."

"You could turn up the air-conditioning."

"We'll all freeze."

"It's a small sacrifice for a bialy," he says.

Jane arrives in the early evening. Guthrie disappears for an hour and returns to the house at seven with a stack of Styrofoam containers filled with barbecue. For an hour, as I gnaw my way through a rack of ribs, I forget all the reasons I have to be miserable.

After dinner Jen puts a candle in a pint of Ben & Jerry's New York Super Fudge Chunk, my favorite flavor. Jane and Guthrie and Jen sing "Happy Birthday." I pay special attention to my father, sitting while the others stand. He doesn't sing. Jen asks my dad whether he wants some ice cream. He says yes.

Because I have a summer birthday, when I was a child I had my parties at the neighborhood pool. My friends and I played Marco Polo in the water and tag in the parking lot. After, the snack bar served burgers and hot dogs and fries and milkshakes. We sat at a long, rectangular table covered in a blue paper tablecloth with the words HAPPY BIRTHDAY stretched across it in neon colors. We wore party hats and blew noisemakers and tossed streamers in the air and at one another. We ate ice cream cake. And then I opened presents while the parents stood around drinking beer and smoking.

I missed Flip terribly during those parties.

I see, now, stuffing spoonfuls of ice cream into my mouth, that he and I have gone opposite ways around a loop of sorts. He was absent when I entered the world. He left just before my sixth birthday, when he was thirty-nine. He missed all my childhood parties. And here we are, at the end of his life, celebrating my thirty-ninth birthday, together.


Guthrie leaves early the next morning. Flip wakes to send him off. After, we sit in the dining room. It's still dark outside. I toast one of the bialys I baked the day before and set a half down in front of my father. I lather mine with cream cheese and eat it. For several minutes he does not touch his. Then he takes a bite and follows it with a sip of tea.

"I think this is the best bialy I've ever had," he says.

Flip's assessment is preposterous.

But also it makes perfect sense. His son baked this bialy, which is probably the last he will ever eat. So I suppose it tastes pretty damn good.


Later in the day a friend calls from California. She offers Jen and me VIP tickets to a Bruce Springsteen concert in San Francisco. We'd have to fly out the next day, spend Saturday at the show, and then return to South Carolina on Sunday. Or I would. Jen would stay at home to take care of the animals and go back to work.

I've been in Clemson for nearly three weeks, most of it in Flip's house. I could use the break. I'm also a lifelong Springsteen fan, and it's not every day someone offers me seats near the stage. I make plane reservations. We watch him for the rest of the day. He seems stable. Jen says his kidneys are probably starting to fail, but it could be weeks at least. At the end of the day we decide to go.

The next morning Flip sits with us at breakfast, though he does not eat. Jen and I chat with Jane. My dad is silent.

Then he says, "Drugs are free in Russia."

We had not been discussing health care policy, so the comment is odd. He does not follow up.

"Is everything all right, Pop?" I say.

He nods.

A few minutes later, to no one in particular, he says, "I hear music in my head."

"What kind of music?" I say.

"Like the radio."

"Is it bothering you?"

"No," he says. He speaks softly, but his words are clear. He's not agitated. "It's kind of nice."

I look at Jen. She asks him about his breathing, whether he's in pain. But he says no. He's fine.

An hour later Jane and Flip wait for us in the kitchen. Flip, dressed in his bathrobe, leans against a counter.

I put my hands on his shoulders and say, "Dad, if you die before I get back, I'm going to kill you."

He smiles.

I hug him and we leave.

*    *    *

Flip kept copies of his published doctoral dissertation, as well as the books of his friends, on a single shelf in his home office. There were Leon Arden's novels and academic works by members of his department and former colleagues.

Next to several copies of my father's only published book, a biography of a congressman named Vito Marcantonio, was a slender volume called *Sex Deviates*. This was not a psychological treatise. Rather, it was pornography. On the cover, a naked man embraces a mostly naked woman. The man's face is obscured, but the woman appears to be having a very nice time. The man is wearing a pinky ring. The book contains one hundred and ninety-two pages of text and ten photographic inserts of the sort you might imagine. It lists no author or publication information.

After noticing how Flip arranged the books in his office, it occurred to me that my father or one of his friends might have written *Sex Deviates*. So, thinking I'd better investigate further, I decided to take the book back to California.

*Sex Deviates* is surprisingly literate and funny and after reading it, I'm convinced it's Flip's doing. The first line says, "When Mimi joined the Pine Cone Players, she never expected to find herself playing with a cone like this one." A man's excited parts are said to be "throbbing like an overworked heart." And it's about the theater: the Pine Cone Players—who are much less interested in satisfying the audience than one another—"had taken on an ambitious project for the start of their summer season, *Redman*, by Arthur Kopout, a dramatic pageant that told the true story of the winning of the West."

It really sounds like Flip.

Also, from the look of the people in the photographs, the book must have come out in the late sixties, which is when my dad was writing fiction. And it contains the sort of references to political issues—interracial romance, feminism, gay rights—you'd hardly expect to find in such a book. *Sex Deviates* is too smart and too tongue-in-cheek and far too weird to have been written by anyone other than my father.

The morning after we return from South Carolina Jen walks into my office looking for something to read. She picks up *Sex Deviates*. I explain. She thumbs through it. She reads to me. I read to her. We retire to the bedroom, leaving the book on my desk. It's one thing to be titillated by something your father may have written. It's another thing altogether to have your father's book see your wife naked.

An hour later Jen and I are napping. The phone rings. Jane is breathless. Flip is dead.

# Epilogue

Forgiveness is where love and justice meet.

—Tony Kushner, *Angels in America*

Flip wanted to be cremated. He told me his will called for his ashes to be dropped from a plane over Clemson University. In fact the will said no such thing. Another time my dad said he wanted his remains spread around Hardin Hall, the building on campus where he spent much of his last thirty years.

When the ashes actually appeared, in a plastic box swathed in a red velvet bag, my brothers and I had second thoughts. We concluded that Flip did not intend his requests to be taken literally. He was simply trying to illustrate how important his work had been to him, how he'd found a home in the history department and in Clemson.

So, rather than risk arrest by the campus police, we gathered, with our stepmother, in a small clearing behind Flip's house. Cullen opened the box and withdrew a plastic bag containing my father's remains. We each spoke a few words. Guthrie sobbed. And then I did, too. We took turns pouring out the ashes around a tree. There were fewer chunks than I expected. I'd heard there would be more chunks.

When it was my turn to handle the bag I tipped it into my palm, letting the ashes collect on my hand and spill over onto the ground. My tears fell down onto my palm, for a moment creating a tiny pool, and then soaking into Flip's remains. It reminded me of my father's inadequately hydrated lavash dough.

We spent the two weeks after Flip died emptying out his house. None of us had a whole lot of time to mourn in South Carolina, so we got to work. Guthrie decided to take the desk my dad built.

It was heavy and unwieldy so it took all three Schaffer sons to get it outside. As we tipped it to hoist it into a rental truck, the top drawer slid out onto the ground. The impact revealed a secret compartment in the drawer, in which Flip had secreted seven hundred dollars along with a key that looked as if it could be for a safe deposit box.

In the three years after my father received his diagnosis, I had many, many conversations with him about his affairs. He never mentioned the drawer.

We spent the next two hours riding around Clemson searching for the right bank, making jokes about what we might find: photographs of a secret family, evidence that he'd been working for the CIA. Finally we found the deposit box, which contained ten thousand dollars in stock certificates. Had we tipped the desk to the left, instead of to the right, the certificates would be there to this day.

Flip made clear, too, that when he died he wanted no ceremonies, no speeches. But his desire to pass without public acknowledgment turned out to be just as hard to fulfill as his wish to spend eternity under a bush next to Hardin Hall. People wanted to gather—colleagues, students, neighbors.

So, a week after his death, we assembled in an auditorium on the Clemson campus for a memorial service. I sat in the third row. The man who hired my father in 1974 to chair Clemson's history department, a ninety-plus, bow-tied Southerner, spoke admiringly of my father's contributions to the school. He called Flip by a single name—*Schafuh*. Leon Arden, who saw Flip for the last time at our dinner at FCI two months before, marveled that while other senior citizens were shopping for walking sticks, Flip had learned to fly airplanes.

During the ceremony I turned back to see if my dad had wandered in. He would have enjoyed it, and he would have found reasons to criticize: this one was too sentimental; that one had her dates wrong.

Afterward, I mingled in a glass-sheathed atrium outside the auditorium, shaking hands, munching on miniature roast beef sandwiches and grapes the size of golf balls. Several times during an hour of thanking people for coming and accepting condolences, mannerly strangers approached me, and in each case, the following exchange occurred.

"And you must be Dylan."

"That's right," I said. By now all four of our hands were clasped, our faces inches apart. "And what's your name?"

The person introduced him or herself, but seemed in a rush to get to a particular point, beyond *I'm so sorry* and *I admired your father a great deal*. The speaker dropped his or her voice a little, seeming to want to keep the matter between us. And it came out pretty much the same every time.

"I just wanted to tell you, I don't think I've ever seen anyone so excited as your father was about your baking class in

New York. When he came back, why, it was like he was a different man. He said it was the highlight of his life. He said it was the best thing he had ever done."

At the time, here's what I thought: Sure, Flip was a changed man. But it wasn't because he learned to make a chewy baguette or how much butter goes into a croissant. During our week in New York he let go the guilt he lugged around for thirty years, the agonizing sense that he could never climb out from beneath the rock he crawled under when he left his children.

I forgave him. That's what happened. I told him I understood, that it was okay, that he was a good father.

Of course, I didn't really think Flip *deserved* pardoning. I believed, as I've mentioned, that some conduct is unforgivable. Some misdeeds ought to stick to you, when you live and when you die.

But I forgave him anyway. I concluded that it makes no difference what he did or how I felt about it or whether he'd earned a pardon. I loved my father and I wasn't about to let him expire with his remorse. In Kushner's formulation, love and justice met, and love prevailed. It was a gift, from me to him.

Or so I thought.

I see now that the truth is more complicated. Flip returned to Clemson and told everyone that the baking class was the highlight of his life. What he didn't say—what he would not have admitted and may not even have known—is that he kept himself going just long enough to go to New York, to make bread, to make amends. He finally talked to me about why he left. He acknowledged how difficult it had been for us to grow up with Cookie.

Perhaps he was pleased that I forgave him, but knowing Flip, I doubt he would have viewed our time together very differently had I told him to go to hell. He said he was sorry. After that, he was free to let go.

Which is not to say that forgiving my father had no meaning. It's just that its significance was mostly for the forgiver. By baking with my dad, walking around New York while he said good-bye to his city, listening to his stories, telling him I loved him despite his faults, forgiving him despite my qualms, and caring for him in the last weeks of his life, I unexpectedly dissolved the anger I'd clung to so doggedly. And so, by the time he died, Flip and I had recovered what we'd lost when he left New York thirty years before.

In a way, I was right. Forgiveness *is* a gift. As it turns out, the gift was to me.

# And One More Thing

*Between dying and dead is a long time.*

—Isaac Bashevis Singer

I loved my father. I love him still. But it should be clear by now that our relationship was not easy. When he called me in November of 2002 and said he wanted to take the baking class at FCI seven months later, I said yes. But I assumed he'd be gone by then. When it was time to go to New York, I was not enthusiastic. I had many reasons not to go. I was busy with law work. I was putting the finishing touches on a book that would become my first published novel. My marriage, in its infancy, was in a difficult place. But I promised, so I went.

And when, weeks later, my brother called and said that Flip was crashing, I might have hired a nurse or asked other family members to go. God knows I would have liked to have saved my starter. But for reasons which include my experience with my friend's mom, love for my dad, the desire to escape the responsibilities of my daily life, and even, I think, the wish to be seen as the sort of person who takes care of his sick father, I went.

What happened between Flip and me, in New York, and then in South Carolina, is our story. I won't say it would work this way for anyone else. Some parents are unreachable.

Some children have been so hurt, are so angry, that building last-minute bridges may be impossible.

But it seems worth saying that spending time with Flip at the end of his life was the best, most enjoyable, most significant, most rewarding thing I have ever done. I know it sounds sentimental, but baking with my father, and then walking him to life's back door to say a final good-bye, was the highlight of my life.

For that reason, I offer this simple, parting advice: Go.

By the way, recently I walked down Spring Street in New York. Just in case you were worried, the rice pudding joint is still going strong.

—D. S., December 2005

Here is the recipe for the bialys I made in South Carolina, the one my dad said resulted in the best bialy he ever tasted. Perhaps he was just being nice. But one thing is for sure: The man knew his bialys.

## For the bread:
2 cups warm (105–115 degree) water
1 package yeast
2 tsp sugar
2 ½ tsp kosher salt
1 ¼ cups bread flour
3 ½ cups all-purpose flour

## For the topping:
1 Tbs vegetable oil
1 ½ tsp poppy seeds
⅓ cup minced onion
½ tsp salt

## Directions:
In a mixing bowl, combine ½ cup warm water, yeast, and sugar and let stand until foamy, about 10 minutes.

Mix remaining (1 ½ cups) water, salt, bread flour, and all-purpose flour into yeast mixture. Knead by hand or in mixer until smooth. You'll end up with a relatively soft dough.

Place dough ball in a greased bowl and turn it over so its greased side faces up. Cover in plastic wrap and let rise until tripled in bulk.

Punch dough down, turn it over, cover, and let rise until doubled.

Punch dough down, cut in half, and roll each half into a cylinder. Cut each into 8 rounds. Lay them flat, cover with a towel and let rest.

Prepare topping by mixing all topping ingredients. Set aside.

Pat dough into flattened rounds (a little higher in middle) about 3 ½ inches in diameter. Place on lightly floured work area, cover with a damp towel and let rise until increased by about half in bulk. This should take about 30 minutes.

Press the bottom of small glass in center of each bialy, to make a deep indentation. Let rise another 15 minutes.

Preheat oven to 425 degrees.

Put bialys on ungreased baking sheets. Place about 1 teaspoon of onion topping in the indentation of each bialy. Bake on upper and lower shelves of the oven for 6 to 7 minutes, then switch the pans and reverse positions of pans (both up and down and front to back) until bialys are evenly browned, about 5 to 6 minutes more.

Cool on racks.

Cut a bialy down the middle and spread the halves with enormous quantities of both cream cheese and butter.

Make grunting sounds while eating.

# Acknowledgments

The acknowledgments is the only part of a book no one edits and no one reviews. It's rather strange, actually.

Readers of early drafts, editors, agents, publicists—they all pay close attention to the text of a book, offering valuable criticisms and guidance. They have opinions about the title, subtitle, book jacket, and flap copy. They send lengthy e-mails about emotional arcs and character development and narrative structure. When the book comes out, reviewers and journalists and bookstore owners and readers from all over creation render judgments on all of the above. I've had several e-mails about the fact that I'm unshaven in my author photo.

But no one has ever commented on my acknowledgments. I suppose hardly anyone reads this section. Which is disappointing, because I go to great lengths to write engaging acknowledgments. But it also means I can say anything I like because who's going to stop me, or even notice?

I mean, why not *acknowledge* that making desserts with cooked fruit makes no sense? Except for the pit, a cherry is a perfect food. It *is* dessert. Why, then, would anyone in his or her right or other sort of mind put cherries inside a piecrust and bake them until they are mushy and vile? Please don't

262 Life, Death & Bialys

even say the word *compote* in my presence. Compote is an abomination.

I would also like to *acknowledge* that while it's true I nearly broke Wendy Brandes's nose in eighth grade, it's also the case that she tickled my neck while I was stretching backward over a chair, and I have issues with my neck, as she well knew. I didn't think it through. I just jerked forward and swiped at whatever or whomever was tickling my neck. And it just happened to be Wendy Brandes.

Let's see. I seem to remember that Dave Eggers acknowledged the United States Postal Service in his memoir. So I hope it won't seem too derivative if I acknowledge my mail carrier, Joan. Joan not only brings the mail and doesn't complain that my dogs bark at her every single day, but also Joan solved a murder up the street a few years ago. I don't imagine many people can say that about their mail carriers.

What else? There's no reason not to *acknowledge* that the Earth is getting warmer, that the death penalty is *dead wrong,* and that women ought to have the right to choose. I'd also like to *acknowledge* that disagreeing with me on these issues does not mean you won't enjoy my book.

I should *acknowledge,* too, that sometimes I imagine that each of my thumbs is the center of a professional basketball team. I run a full court game up and down my desk and work up quite a sweat in the process.

I feel certain that like everyone else at the wonderful publishing house of Bloomsbury, my editor, Colin Dickerman, won't read this section. Thus, I can be totally honest and *acknowledge* that Colin is a brave and sensitive soul who took a considerable leap of faith on this book; also he is the best-looking man in the publishing business.

Additionally, I would like to *acknowledge* the following titles that I or someone else thought of but were rejected by readers, editors, or other experts:

Flip
Flip & Me
Me & Flip
Baking with Flip
Our Daily Bialy
The Last Bialy
The Funniest Book About Death & Bialys Ever
Don't Forget the Bialys
All You Knead
My Father's Time of Knead
A Friend in Knead
Time to Knead
Knead, Punch, Score
On His Way to Paradise, My Father Stopped for Bialys
Papa Had a Rolling Pin

Without assistance of all sorts from my friend Hilary Liftin, my agent, Lydia Wills, and my brother Cullen Schaffer, it is fair to say that while I might have written these acknowledgments, you would not be reading them. So, in a sense, these three people are the ones to blame if you hate these acknowledgments. Come to think of it, they are pretty much responsible for the fact that you paid good money for this book, so if you have complaints, e-mail me and I'll send you their home numbers.

Others partially to blame: David Agretelis, Leon Arden, Yvette Banek, Marian Brown, Lara Carrigan, Nancy Cohen,

Dave Cronin, Sabrina Farber, Alona Fryman, Tim Halbur, Laure Hansen, John Hansen, Amy Heibel, Jane Herndon, Sally Hunt, Lizzy Klein, Al Menaster, Hannah Rosen, Guthrie Schaffer, Anschel Schaffer-Cohen, Lisa Schiffman, and Greg Villepique.

I cannot adequately *acknowledge* or thank the generous and patient and kind-hearted chefs—Hans Welker and Caterina Liviakis—or students in the June 2003 French Culinary Institute's Artisanal Baking class. So I won't.

Dr. Jennifer Dykes, a brilliant and funny and stunningly beautiful woman, married me and lives with me. I do not understand how this happened. But, since the opportunity arises here, I'll *acknowledge* that I'm a pain in the ass and that I don't deserve her.

My father, Flip Schaffer, is dead, which is news to you only if you are reading the acknowledgments first, and in that case I have no sympathy for you because I consider that to be cheating. Anyway, he's dead, but does that mean he doesn't deserve acknowledging? He paid for the baking class. He put up with my incessant questioning. He even told the truth about some important stuff, which could not have been easy for him. So, in conclusion, I would like to *acknowledge* that despite his many deficiencies, I could not possibly have loved my father any more.